"*If You Only Knew: A Book of Healing Letters* is a heartfelt treasure trove of wisdom, vulnerability, and grace. Through these intimate and beautifully written letters, Junie Swadron reminds us of the healing power of truth, love, and authentic connection. This book is a gentle invitation to return to the sacred art of letter writing and to the deeper knowing of our own hearts. Junie's words are soul medicine."

~ Marci Shimoff, #1 NY Times bestselling author of Happy for No Reason and Chicken Soup for the Woman's Soul

If You Only Knew...

A Book of Healing Letters

May the letters you write keep or release,
carry you ever closer to peace.
May your words always lead you home to yourself.

Junie Swadron

eBook ISBN: 978-1-965761-78-6
Paperback ISBN: 978-1-965761-79-3
Ingram Spark: ISBN: 978-1-965761-80-9
Library of Congress Control Number: 2025922533

Editor: Megan McConnell – www.thelastline.ca
Cover Design: Emily Edge
Interior Design: Marigold 2K
Publisher: Spotlight Publishing House™
https://spotlightpublishinghouse.com

Dedication

Without the presence of God's love in my life, I can't fathom where I might be today. The unmistakable benevolence that holds me in my darkest hours and the unimaginable joy that fills me when inspiration hits is beyond description. Between these extremes is the place where I rest, knowing the Source of Infinite Love is available to me in every moment. For this, I am eternally grateful.

I dedicate this book to my late parents, Minnie and Jimmie Swadron, who loved me the best way they knew how, and sometimes, it was with love beyond measure.

Finally, I dedicate this book to the countless people who have shown up since my cancer diagnosis with their unconditional loving-kindness. I am blown away by this avalanche of love.

Content Disclaimer

This book contains personal stories of healing, including one letter that describes experiences of childhood and adolescent sexual abuse. The language in this section is graphic and may be triggering for some readers. Please take care of yourself as you read. If you feel overwhelmed, you may choose to skip that section or return to it when you feel ready.

The stories are shared with the intention of breaking silence, offering truth, and supporting healing. If you have experienced similar trauma and need support, please consider reaching out to a trusted friend, counselor, or a local crisis support service.

Sincerely,

Junie

Contents

Acknowledgements

This book would not exist without the love, encouragement, and patience of so many people who have walked beside me on this journey.

To my family, who have held me in both my brightest and darkest moments—you are the roots and the branches of my life. To my family of friends, those kindred spirits who have become as close as kin, thank you for reminding me that love is not limited by blood, but is grown in the soil of trust and shared experience.

To my clients and former students, who entrusted me with your stories and healing journeys—your courage has inspired me to keep writing, keep teaching, and keep showing up. You are part of every word on these pages.

To my dear friend and editor, Megan, who helped shape my words into the story I most needed to tell—thank you for believing in me, for holding space for my truth, and for bringing your heart and brilliance to this book. I could not have done this without you.

And finally, to every person who has ever written or longed to write a letter of healing: may this book be a companion on your path, and may you discover the power of your own words.

Forward

There are words we speak and words we never say. There are letters written in ink and letters carried only in the quiet chambers of the heart. This book holds both.

If You Only Knew: A Book of Healing Letters is a collection of truths, whispered and shouted, offered and withheld, fragile and fierce. Each letter is a doorway into one woman's journey of love, loss, forgiveness, and becoming. And yet, as you read, you may find that these letters do not belong to her alone. They belong to all of us who have ever longed to say what could not be said.

Created in the tender threshold of hospice, these pages are woven from courage. They remind us that healing is not only found in cures, but in honesty. Not only in holding on, but also in letting go.

May you enter this book gently. May the letters stir your own, waiting to be written. And may you discover, in the act of reading, that you too are part of this tapestry of healing words.

Introduction

Dearest Reader,
  if you only knew...

Thank you for choosing to read this book, a compilation of letters and stories I have written to people who have significantly impacted my life and, therefore, shaped it in myriad ways.

It is my hope that these letters speak to your heart as I wrote them from the bottom of mine. Although the content may or may not be relatable to your own personal life stories, I believe they will spark the shared humanity in all of us. An important motivation for writing this book of letters is to reinstate the art and joy of letter writing to the world! To bring back something that had been sacred for centuries before modern technology replaced it.

Today, and especially over the past two decades, email has taken over from the art of letter writing. Before computers, letters were the common way people around the world spoke with their loved ones. Long-distance phone calls were far too expensive when I was a child, whereas you could send a whole letter to practically anywhere in the world with a 4-cent stamp!

Besides the economic benefit, the enormous benefit of heartfelt warmth and well-being cannot be quantified. How do you measure how it feels to sit down at your desk with a hot cup of tea, pick out a favourite writing pen, and a lovely piece of stationery, and begin writing to someone you love? And then, remember, or imagine, if you will, being the recipient of such a letter, a letter written especially and only to you that extends such love and kindness.

I, and I am sure thousands of others like me, remember how incredibly special the ritual of handwriting letters and receiving them in kind felt. When I sit down to write a letter, there is no one else that exists—just me and my beloved friend, lover, teacher, grandparent. In *If You Only Knew: A Book of Healing Letters*, I also write to places, God, and even Death. There are no limits to who you can write a letter to, or even where.

For me, the ritual begins like this: I sip my tea at my desk or cozy up on my bed with pillows stacked behind me and then I start writing. Time disappears. When I have finished writing and put my pen down, I read it back, feeling very satisfied—my heart happy with the contents. I then carefully place my letter in an envelope, put a stamp on it, and walk to the red mailbox—often kissing it before excitedly dropping it into the slot.

Now, the anticipation began. Oh yes. First, I think about how my friend will feel once it arrives. I imagine her coveting it to her heart once she gets it, and then taking the time to read every word, and possibly reading it again because it is filled with the kinds of sentiments only best friends share, as well as the latest news and maybe even a joke or two.

And then comes the next part... waiting. Waiting for the arrival of her letter and checking the mailbox each day. Nope, not today. The next day, nope, not today. But then the day comes when her letter arrives and, just like I imagine it with my friend, I covet the letter, go into the kitchen, fire up the kettle for a cup of tea, then take the letter and tea to my bedroom, and close the door so I can be completely alone.

Carefully opening the envelope, I see my name...

Dearest Junie,

I read every word as though it were manna from heaven; the excitement building knowing how our hearts have touched one another across the miles, and before long, another letter ensued.

The time it takes for a letter to be written, sent, received, and then sent back can take weeks, even months, and the anticipation grows with each peek into my mailbox. Receiving a letter back is, for me, like winning the lottery!

Why do I think letter and story writing is important, especially now? Because the world suffers from loneliness. A letter, which is a tactile, breathing entity of connection from one heart to another, is life-sustaining.

I regret that this book did not come out during COVID, when the entire world was in lockdown, where we could not visit our friends and relatives in their homes, and worse, were not allowed to visit them in the hospital or nursing homes. I can only imagine the joy that a letter would have brought to these individuals who were sick and all alone, except for the nursing staff, to care for their physical needs.

Many had devices where they could get messages—and we all have those—and will continue to. Yes, emails are okay, and I am thankful for them, but they cannot be compared to the ritual of letter writing.

Emails, texts, and similar forms of communication are convenient, and we have all grown accustomed to writing them and expecting a response within the same day, or even within minutes. I certainly do not expect letters would or ever could replace emails and texts. It would be comparing apples and oranges.

Letters are in a category of their own. They require time, and they require the kind of communication that stems from our soul's longing to connect... and they provide just that.

As you read the following letters, I hope they will prompt you to think about someone you care about and will inspire you to pick up your pen and write from your heart. You do not need to follow my version of it. You can write from anywhere you like—a coffee shop, a library, on your bed, or sofa.

Where you write your letter does not matter. What matters is how awesome you are going to feel writing it, sending it, and knowing the joy of excited anticipation as you await a response.

The letters you are about to read are my letters of love to people who have shaped my life, whether they came as earth angels, lifting me when I needed lifting, or people who forced me to grow, who taught me things about myself that perhaps I would not have learned in any other way.

There are letters of joy, thank-you notes, stories, and expressions of appreciation to teachers and mentors. Letters of self-discovery and letters to God. Letters of intimacy and letters just for me that do not require a stamp but bear witness to a me who had a longing to write them.

Several of these letters are to people who have died, and I am asking for forgiveness beyond the veil. Writing allowed me to say it all without holding anything back. Things I wished I had been able to say while they were alive but could not, such as in my letter to Deborah Millar, or my letter to my Boobie, long after her death, in which I wrote her a story of how I wish it had been. These letters and stories are laden with regrets and deep love, which I had carried in my heart, sometimes for decades.

I begin the journey of *If You Only Knew* with the two letters that are the genesis for this book. The first letter is one I wrote to my dear friend, Rena, my Year of Miracles Mentor Coach, who was so inspired by my idea of sharing the lost art of letter writing that she offered to connect me with Marci Shirmoff, the creator of Your Year of Miracles and the author of *Chicken Soup for the Woman's Soul.* Sharing my long-time vision for *If You Only Knew* helped me to see how possible it was to bring it into the world, even as I reside in Hospice, praying for another miracle—that of walking out of here, healthy and whole once again.

Writing provides closure and a deep understanding that not only have I been forgiven, but I have also forgiven myself for simply being human and doing the best that I could have at the time. And that there is no separation at all when love is fully present. It is never too late to say we are sorry. It is never too late to open ourselves to the love that is inherent within us, the love that can spread like wildflowers across fields and meadows and everywhere, when we write from our core, when we write from the pure essence of love.

All blessings and love,

Junie

If You Only Knew...
A Book of Healing Letters

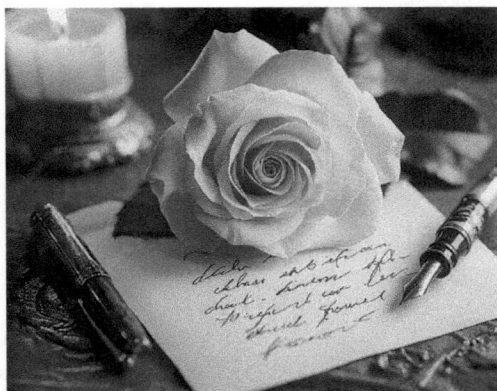

Letters are the echoes of our soul's voice;
may yours always guide you toward the light within.

November 7, 2024

Dearest Rena,
    if you only knew...

I can't thank you enough for your enthusiastic willingness to share my book, *If You Only Knew: A Book of Healing Letters,* with Marci Schimoff. It would be an absolute miracle come true if she hears how you personally received my material, as I shared it with you, and takes it into her heart in the same way.

I truly believe that this latest book, my eighth, will be pivotal in helping to reduce what I believe to be the most prevalent and frightening disease on the planet: loneliness.

It is my supreme wish that this book will inspire the art of letter writing again—especially with young people who, in many cases, are not taught cursive handwriting in school and therefore cannot read unless it is computer-generated! Technology can never take over the very essence of what makes us human—the need to connect, the need to give and receive love. We've all become increasingly dependent on devices these days, and it's heartbreaking to think that many young people today don't know how to communicate beyond the screen.

When readers see the value of writing letters, which is all spelled out in my introduction, which I have attached to this email, I hope they will be inspired to pick up their pen and write a letter to someone they love, admire, miss, cherish, or simply 'just because.'

I believe with all my heart that my book can move countless others—just like the original *Chicken Soup for the Soul* did. Jack Canfield and Mark Victor Hansen state that they never realized when they wrote that first book that it would achieve the massive success it did.

"Never, in Jack and Mark's wildest dreams, had they imagined what the book would become. *Chicken Soup for the Soul* turned into one of the most popular and loved books ever published, selling 11 million copies around the world. Readers asked for more stories, so we published a "second helping" of *Chicken Soup for the Soul* and a third after that. Today, we've published more than 250 books, which have become the best-selling trade paperback book series of all time."

In the same article above, Jack Canfield and Mark Victor Hansen state:

"We started in 1993 with a simple idea: that people could help each other by sharing stories about their lives."

Now that these two visionaries, Jack and Mark, along with our dear Marci, who had the brilliant idea for *Chicken Soup for the Women's Soul*, have paved the way for other writers, healers, and changemakers like me. I feel confident that my book can obtain the same kind of global success.

My idea for this book, in its own way, stems from the same seed that Jack and Mark planted years ago—simply sharing healing stories, and in my case, written in letter form—will profoundly change people's lives for the better.

Thank you, Rena, for your beautiful response after listening to me read Davida's letter to you. Davida shaped my life in ways that brought me to a level of success I couldn't have achieved without her encouragement to go back to school. I only wish I could have told her this while she was still alive.

Hence my letter: "Dearest Davida, if you only knew..."

I have attached this letter along with two others, both in written and audio form, for you to enjoy and forward to Marci with your comments. There are many more written that can be shared as well, but these will give a good sense. Hmm, I just decided in the spur of the moment to include one more letter, "Dearest Cancer," which I recently transcribed from my journal. I am deeply grateful that God answered my most heartfelt prayer: to let me live! And live as an instrument of kindness and grace.

By the way, in one of my author mentorship programs, I asked some of my students to write letters to people in their lives that could be included in future *If You Only Knew* books, and I have some of them ready to submit if Marci wants to read them. Additionally, on Monday, I asked participants at the seniors' home where I facilitate memoir writing to write a letter to someone who has positively impacted their life. They did, and as you can imagine, they are beautiful. Some of them have agreed to let me send them to Marci, should she want to see some samples of what others write. See, the book has already got a following 😊

You also asked me to send you my intentions...

You, Rena, being a connector—bringing this letter to Marci and having her see it the same way I do and being willing to help me get it into the world—would be the magic and the miracle I am praying for!

Here are my miracle intentions and prayers as though they have already come to pass. I would be so grateful if you could supercharge them for me.

Thank you!

Junie

Part 1

Marci received the package that Rena sent her, all about my book of letters, and she was so excited that she replied to Rena immediately! She told Rena that she wanted to set up a meeting with me right away. That she loved the idea. She absolutely sees my book becoming a huge international success and evolving into a large and happy series of books, just like *Chicken Soup for the Soul* has done.

Part 2

On the spot, during our conversation, Marci said an enthusiastic YES! to endorsing it and helping me get it out in the world in a big way!

She sent my book to her publisher, who got in touch with me immediately. We worked together on the cover (where Marci's endorsement stands out!), then they worked on the interior layout, etc. They worked together with me as though it were their very own book, with incredible passion and enthusiasm, and the process was seamless. When I was asked if writing the book was a labour of love, I said you can remove the word labour. It was simply love in action! And the part that was the magic icing on this already 5-Star Miracle-Layered Cake: I didn't have to pay a nickel for the publishing, distribution, and the like. I just needed to write the book!

It was paid by a scholarship fund that Marci had already set up for authors whom she deemed worthy of having their books published but didn't have the financial means to produce them first-class. These are books that will make a stunning difference in touching people's lives. Wow!!! I'm still pinching myself.

Part 3

My book has reached No. 1 on the New York Times Bestseller List. OMG!!! I have no words. This woman, me, who has more words than anyone else I know, is entirely speechless.

Part 4

During our initial conversation, Marci showed a genuine interest in getting to know me beyond my latest book. Despite her crazy-busy schedule, she took the time out for "me." Wow!!!

She wanted to know more about my life journey. I told her how my early beginnings were highly traumatic, resulting in what seemed like a revolving door in and out of mental institutions. Yet, like the phoenix, I spread my wings wide, rose high above the identity of someone with mental illness, transformed the traumatic beginnings, and have become a powerful advocate for mental health. She then invited me to be a guest on her Happiness for No Reason Podcast. Since our magnificent interview, I have been getting calls to be a guest on other podcasts hosted by worldwide influencers and changemakers! Wow!!!

I can't help but live by Helen Keller's quote: "One can never consent to creep when one has an impulse to soar!"

My programs, books, and international talks ignite the impulse to soar in everyone who experiences them!

This is the life I have dreamed myself in for so many years... to be counted among leaders who have nothing in the way of stopping themselves from being the Spark of God that they are! I am now walking among them, financially free, creating outrageous abundance through my love and service, and I have also called in the man of my dreams. Yes... This God, or something better. But seriously? Can it get better than this!!! I am 75 years young... an age where so many have given up and feel it's their last chapter. Me... I've only just begun!

Once again, I am absolutely speechless. The only thing I can think to say is the two words that come from the wisdom of Meister Eckhart: "If the only prayer you ever say in your entire life is Thank You, it would be enough." I would say it in every language ever spoken.

Thank you, God! Thank you, Marci! Thank you, Rena! And thank you, to myself, for being the brave woman you are and never giving up.

Thank you to every person who has ever come into my life, who has helped me to believe in myself, allowing me to put down another pebble on my path toward doing God's work on this planet. Thank you to every celestial angel who has walked beside me, even when I haven't a clue that they are there. And still...

I am truly blessed. And so it is!

FOUNDATION:

I TRUST IN THE UNIVERSE

All Blessings and Gratitude,

Junie

November 7, 2024

Dearest Marci,
   if only you knew…

Re: If You Only Knew: A Book of Healing Letters

I am sending this letter to you via Rena Boone, who is my Year of Miracles Momentum Coach, and whom I have fallen in love with! She's absolutely Divine! A gift from God! I had a "light bulb moment" when I realized Rena would be someone who could reach you much faster than I could on my own. So, I shared my idea with her, and after she listened (the way she listens—with every part of her awake and receptive), she had no hesitation in agreeing to pass on her experience of it. I am absolutely thrilled with Rena's response, and it is my greatest hope that you receive what I am offering, in kind. ☺

   First, Marci, I want to thank you with all my heart, for "A Year of Miracles"—for having that brilliant idea, sharing it with your most amazing co-hearts, and bringing it to life the way you do again and again… in YOM, in your books *Happy For No Reason* and *Love For No Reason*, in your podcast interviews, in your philanthropic work, and in your personal life. You are the same person behind the scenes as in front of them. I haven't been behind the scenes with you yet, but I know this in my heart to be 100% true. Integrity rules your heart and every breath you take, so of course, they would be synonymous.

   I want you to know that you, your treasured teammates in YOM, and the YOM community have fueled my life and have been my lifeline for almost two years since I first discovered you and registered in 2023.

At that time, I had a rare form of cancer, was still going through treatment, could hardly get out of bed, and the doctors were not sure that I would recover. Today I am 100% cancer-free!!! And I am possibly the most humble and grateful person on the planet, humbly spoken, of course 😊

I am also fully back into the spirit of life and doing the work I love, even though I lost six friends to cancer this year. The grief has been immeasurable. It seemed that every month, I was attending another celebration of life or funeral service for someone I loved deeply. Also, in January this year, my husband left me, and the shock of that left me gasping for my life. I fell into the dark night of the soul from which I did not think I would return.

Using my resiliency skills, I reached out and I reached in and healed whatever was needing healing, and I let go in love, and since then, my life has changed significantly. My former husband and I have since come together as friends of the heart—and we are both blessing each other on our individual journeys forward.

It is no coincidence that my vibrant health has much to do with what YOM offers. No matter how ill I felt or how dark it was, I turned on every offering you and your team gave. It became a necessary lifeline for me. I can never thank you enough, Marci!

The reason for this letter is that I am writing a book, and I would love for you to consider endorsing it. I also dream of collaborating with you to bring it out into the world. It is my intention to reach countless others, so they, too, will experience the power of healing in the way I describe in my book. I know it is a huge ask, and yet, if I don't ask, I'd be letting myself down. After all, you could say "Yes!"

I had a similar ask when I wrote my first book in 2009. At that time, I found the courage after an NDE (near-death experience), and waking up in a state of Grace, to write to Julia Cameron and ask her if she would kindly endorse my book, *Re-Write Your Life, A Transformational Guide to Writing and Healing the Stories of Our Lives*. I revered Julia Cameron, and I had been facilitating a support group for her book, *The Artist's Way*, for fifteen years.

Still, she didn't know me from Adam, or Mary or Sue! Yet, two weeks after I sent my request to her publisher, her publisher wrote back to me that Julia Cameron wanted to read my manuscript. OMG! Two weeks after that, on my 60th birthday, no less, I received this endorsement.

> "Junie Swadron is both a guide and a muse. Her book is a bright lantern, illuminating the often dark and tricky terrain of the soul. Grounded in personal experience, her techniques catalyze the deep authenticity possible to us all."
> —Julia Cameron, Author of *The Artist's Way*

Now, it's fifteen years later, I have published six additional books, and at 75 years young, I am reaching out to you, Marci.

Why you? Not just because I love you and you are a world leader with an extensive reach, and because you are a number one award-winning author—it's because I believe what I am about to share with you will resonate in kind.

My book, *If You Only Knew: A Book of Healing Letters*, is similar to the *Chicken Soup for the Soul* series in that it can evolve into multiple books stemming from my original work.

The primary motivation for this book is to help mitigate one of the most prevalent diseases on the planet, loneliness. When I first started writing these letters, that wasn't the motivation. It was to speak with full abandon to people who helped shape my life. Some came as earth angels when I really needed one. Others came as human 2x4s, forcing me to grow, and grow; I did. Both, I equally thank. I came to realize that there are two other strong motivations for getting this book out into the world. The second is so that people who are still holding onto something they haven't had the courage to say in person can find deep inner peace by putting it in a heartfelt letter. The third motivation is to reinstate the art of letter writing.

Having been born during an era of letters as a common way to communicate, I know the unquantifiable value they bring to both the letter writer and to the one who receives it. Opening such a letter is an immediate tactile, visceral representation of the person you love, as though they are right there in the room with you.

Nothing else exists in this present moment when you read their words of love that fill up the pages just for you and you alone.

I only wish my book could have been published during COVID, when we couldn't visit our loved ones in hospitals and nursing homes. Can you imagine the delight people in these places would have felt to receive a letter from their loved ones? Their partner, mom or dad, son or daughter, best friend, or cousin? Well, it's never too late to spread love, as you, the author of *Love for No Reason*, know without question.

Please read the introduction to my book, which provides a deeper explanation of why this book means so much to me. As well, I have attached samples of three letters I wrote, both in written and audio form.

Oh, Marci, it would be the biggest miracle come true if you were to see the value of what I am offering and would want to endorse it, helping me get it out into the world like only you—as the author of *Chicken Soup for the Women's Soul*—could do.

I remember you sharing your story that when you had the idea for that book—also a light-bulb moment! —you happened to be at a Vipassana silent retreat where you couldn't talk. You could hardly wait for it to end so you could call Jack Canfield and share your inspired idea with him. I can only imagine your absolute thrill and delight when he said, YES!... and the rest is beautiful history

As Your Year of Miracles is all about manifesting the biggest dreams that we can imagine for ourselves, well, this is the one I covet the most! I am reaching out to you to help me know what it is like to have a miracle of this calibre come true!

I hope you see its value to countless people in the same way that I do. Thank you so much, Marci, for your loving consideration.

All blessings and gratitude,

Junie

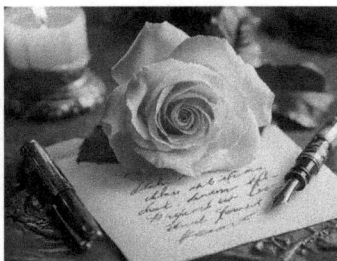

Dear Reader,

This letter is to Davida, my beloved friend and mentor, whose laughter, intellect, and love shaped my life in ways I can never repay. Though she is no longer with us, her spirit lingers in every memory, every lesson, and every shared moment of joy. Writing to her now, I am raw, open, and unshielded, revisiting a friendship that spanned decades and bridged distance, loss, and time. In these words, I honor her, celebrate her, and continue the conversation that never truly ended.

Love,

Junie

Dearest Davida,
  if you only knew...

T oday is August 11ᵗʰ, and if you were still alive today, this would be your birthday. And, more than likely, we would be celebrating it in one of the many ways that you loved to celebrate. You were the "quintessential Leo."

You loved bravado, good taste, and a good party! One of my favourite parties was when you asked everyone to bring something that represented something we loved. I made you the Cat Jam Jazz/ Blues Band set on a two-tiered cardboard box that I painted purple. It was equipped with a mirrored dance floor with dancers and musicians—all cats, of course—and made with pipe cleaners, and it was the most fun project I had ever worked on! I mean, it did represent things I loved and continue to love—music, dance, and cats!

And how I loved you for as long as our friendship was alive... and still. I have so many things I want to tell you. I hope you can hear me now. What was buried so deeply in a protective boulder so that I wouldn't shatter into rock, then crumble into sand, erupted last night in a shocking blast of dynamite.

There is no protective cover now—I come to you raw—my soul fully exposed... and in memory I see you there when you opened your door as you had for two decades of our lives, always dressed to the nines—larger than life—all 5 ft 10 of you and your wild flaming red hair and our hugs which sometimes felt more like visits, just as often got cut short by the excitement of what we were about to share... the latest news coupled with gossip and giggles, disappointments and tears as we cared and we shared and paired as no other in our lives at that time. And even with daily visits when we lived in the same building or weekly visits when we didn't, we came to each other as brand new every time.

And then the day came that I dreaded, the day I had to tell you my news that I was moving to the West Coast—to the place my soul had longed to be for thirty years—and I watched as your face went pale as you attempted a smile and told me how happy you were for me. And although you may have been, it was just too damn hard for you... not again... not again... too many endings to bear. You couldn't stand the pain of another person you loved leaving you. You chose your few friends carefully, and with any perceived threat, you would leave them before they could leave you. So, you withdrew from me... and then withdrew even more, and you built walls to protect your heart, which left my heart broken so deep in despair that eventually I copied you and built my own walls to cover a loss that no words could comfort.

And then Carla's call one week ago; 5:30 in the morning. "Sorry to wake you. June, but I knew you would want to know. Davida died yesterday morning." And I shrieked, "NO!" I hung up the phone with tears streaming down my face and grabbed my journal and madly scribbled twenty-two pages of heartbreak. But it wasn't enough—there was more. I was driven now; the dam had burst. The rock was now sand, and before it was swallowed by the sea, I had to embody it all.

You, me, us... I found the file that carried the remnants of our life—almost too heavy to carry filled with all the cards, letters, poetry, and paintings that I could never throw out, and even though it split my heart open to be with all these memories that spoke our story of love and friendship—a love that was supposed to last forever, no matter where our geography took us—I needed to remember everyone. I needed to get drunk on your essence. So, what I always wanted to tell you, Davida, is this: I have always missed you and I do still.

So here we are, meeting again... a meeting beyond the veil. But it's a transparent veil, and I can see your eyes. I can almost touch you.

You know, I looked at your painting the other night before I went to bed. It has been hanging on my wall since I moved here three years ago and has hung in every home I've ever lived since you gave it to me for my 40th birthday—twenty-one years after we met. I looked at it that night as though I was looking at it for the very first time... and it was curious. I wondered if I should keep it there. Maybe I should take it down. After all, you weren't in my life anymore. The friendship was long over. But as I stood there taking in the brilliant colors of every flower on the canvas, so vivid I could almost smell their fragrance and the monarch butterfly finding its nectar in the calla lily, a sadness washed over me... but also a love so pure that I knew I couldn't, and I wouldn't take it down.

We haven't spoken in about four years—no, it's probably been seven or eight, but I want to lie, I want to believe that it never happened at all. That we spoke every day. That you did wish me well, that you withstood the geographical distance between us and you changed your adamant refusal to use email, and we'd talk on the phone, and you'd come to visit me, and I'd show you what drew me to this wonderous land, and I'd make you my first priority on every return to Toronto. And we'd still be holding hands across the miles... to this very day... or at least 'til the day you died. And now you've left me. You've left me! As long as I knew you were alive, there was always a tinge of hope that we'd find our way back to one another. You were not just my friend; you were my mentor. I could never repay you for what you taught me.

I was only twenty-eight. You were thirty when we met in Montreal, and I must admit that I was intimidated by you. Intimidated by your worldliness, your stately beauty, self-assurance, intellect, sophistication, passion for theatre and painting, Judaism, and your poetry... oh yes, your poetry... which is what bound us together in the first place. We began to meet regularly and read each other our poetry.

Mine always felt insignificant compared to yours. Yours were filled with stunning imagery, metaphor, never superfluous. You used words I had never heard of, but I knew what they meant because my heart understood. And somehow my poetry moved you... or perhaps it was my ability to be vulnerable and open my heart on the page, not in a sophisticated way, but in a real way that made you love me. Your poetry became your medicine as you blasted through your world in a flurry of activity, at the hub of Montreal's largest cultural events.

You immersed yourself completely so that you wouldn't feel the unspeakable loss of Leo's death. It happened only a year before I met you, but it took months for you to share the details with me. Until then, you assumed the Jacqueline Kennedy stance of holding your head high, dignified. You put a padlock on the part of your heart that died the day that he did.

There you were, on vacation in Mexico with your best friends, celebrating your sixth anniversary, when suddenly he keeled over on the dance floor and was dead by the time he hit the ground. A brain aneurysm. Six months later, your other beloved best friend, your father, died. The man you worshipped. The man who taught you the richness of life. The one with whom you shared Torah and philosophy, literature, and politics. The one who instilled in you a love and thirst for knowledge, where learning became as essential as breathing. And you brought this learning to your students for thirty years.

"Davida's Place, Where Learning Is Fun!" Your private tutorial and remediation academy. The place for kids to come after school to work on the subjects they couldn't pass. The students that the teachers, parents, and psychologists believed would never know academic achievement, having failed year after year. But not you. You threw away all the so-called professional reports and found the soul of every child and loved them back to life. Little by little, they began to stand taller, and their grades improved until they aced them and went on to university. That wasn't a one-time deal. That was the norm. And it wasn't just the kids. It was me too. Without your encouragement, love, mentorship, and tutelage, I would never have gone back to school. You saw my intelligence and ability when I could not. You told me I was an excellent writer when you read my papers, and you were not one to compliment unless it was truly deserved. And you guided me to the halls of York University, and your joy was unsurpassed with each of my successes.

It was during that time that we lived in the same apartment building. We would often spend our Saturday or Sunday nights playing Scrabble, listening to Leonard Cohen, Laura Nyro, Janis Ian, Carol King, The Beatles, Joni Mitchel, and filling the ashtray with cigarette after cigarette. On one such occasion, I was in one of my depressed states and felt unsafe going down the stairwell to my apartment after midnight, and I asked if you would walk me down.

You looked at me with my hair in curlers, my pink rabbit pajamas with the bunny ears hood, and remarked with a straight face and meaning every word, "June, you are singularly unattractive. You needn't worry." That cracked me up, and I went skipping down the stairs. I loved your humor. In fact, I loved and cherished everything about you.

Even after you told me that our friendship was over and to please stop calling you, I couldn't. So, I sent you a video of my play, *Madness, Masks and Miracles*, and you wrote me a letter that praised the writing, the performance, and the brilliance of it, and your words meant more to me than any of the other accolades I received. So, Davida, if you were here, and of course you are, with all my heart, I thank you. I thank you for the hugs and the love, the Scrabble games, the picnics, the camping trips, the Passover Seder dinners, and oh my goodness... I could go on forever, couldn't I?

And here you are right now beside me. Just as you were the night I stood and looked at your painting. You came to tell me all is forgiven and that you always loved me, too. You came to tell me you are at peace... and there is nothing that I would ever want more for you. I love you, my forever friend.

Shalom.
Baruch ha'shem.

Junie

Dear Reader,

This is a letter to Kevin, a man I met by chance one night along Dallas Road, not long after his release from prison. Our brief encounters stirred something in me—curiosity, fear, compassion, and the old longing to save others. More than anything, though, Kevin reflected to me the question I had carried for so long: was I June, hardened and closed, or Junie, soft and open-hearted? In writing to him, I found that the answer was not about who he was, but about who I was finally becoming.

Love,

Junie

Dearest Kevin,
    if you only knew...

I keep waiting for some magical opening, searching for a jump off point... somewhere where an opening into the abyss is safe—safe to fall... fall for good... a fall into a place where the words can tumble beyond words, beyond thoughts, beyond this unnameable reality of me—June Darling Swadron... since sometime a year ago saying, no... it's Junie.

"Don't call me June." What's that about? Even when the people who love me unconditionally, like Val, when she calls me June, instead of her affectionate, Junie Bean... or when Trish, who is slipping more every day... cancer ravaging her body now... telling me on the phone two days ago that we are soul sisters—Trish, eighty-something... and me... well, it won't take long to catch up to eighty-something... shit—63... could that really be?

But I'm getting off topic. That's another story... again. Don't want to go there now.

Want to talk about being called June—even when the people who say the name lovingly—something inside me goes crunch... like the sound your boot makes when you walk over the puddle of water that froze overnight. I love the sound really, but in this case, it's like bones crunching in on themselves. It's as if I want to find the Junie who died. The one who was called Junie... with affection... who was given the benefit of the doubt by the people who mattered.

Who was that girl, and who was it that mattered? I don't know, but somewhere along the line, she adopted June... that stern, mean, angry, unforgiving voice that seized my throat and strangled the words before they were even born. Yet I went on to live as her. I was her. I became the frozen voice... disguised in the voice of love to others while my own, my own sweet, innocent, loving Junie, got buried under a wall of cement.

So, who did you meet, Kevin? Did I show up as June, or Junie? Sixty-three... almost 64. Not that that mattered to you. But age is important for what it says about a person. Like John's daughter at the pool today—proudly announcing, "I'm four years old! Soon I'll be four and a half!" Big, wide smile, long blond curls. Declaring her pride to be almost a half number bigger... no concept of what those numbers mean.

I had long blond curls once. I was four and almost four and a half years old. I honestly have no recollection. My life seems to have started on Neptune Drive—and I was already seven. Even after that, life was sketchy.

I'm reading a book that is grabbing my throat... more violence than I expected. It didn't start off that way. Started off as a man on the run... escaped to India and fully embraced Bombay as though it was his ancestral home... becoming one with the people of the slums and... oh my, to write like he does.

And I thought that it was a coincidence, even knowing there's no such thing—coincidence, that is—that I'm reading a book about a criminal who did twenty years just like you, Kevin, and then pushing a wrong button on my play list brings up Johnny cash singing "Fulsome Prison," and different things, here and there, that I can't remember—but connection to prison, leading me toward my latest obsession, YOU.

Kevin... Kevin. You, the man whom I met months ago. When? September? October? I don't know but it was late. It was dark along Dallas Road. I had fought with my brother, Howard, and left my apartment to walk off my frustration and anger. I walked longer and farther than I thought I would—quite dark now to be walking along the edges of Dallas Rd, but I felt better having walked. Then, five minutes from home, I almost didn't notice a man ahead of me on the sidewalk.

You said, "Do you see that light out there?" And I looked to where you were looking and didn't. So, you pointed it out... I think it was green... I guess it was a light for the ships to see each other, or a lighthouse or something. I didn't know much about what you were talking about, but your honest enthusiasm and curiosity were refreshing. So, I stayed, and we talked longer—crossing the street to look over the rails that separated us from the sea. I can't remember everything we talked about, but what stands out is the quality I sensed while you were talking. There was an excitement—a joy, like a child discovering something for the first time... an innocence, which is funny when I think of it now, considering you told me moments later that you had just come out of Williams Head prison just a day or two prior.

I liked talking to you. I told you about my brother and the argument we just had. You seemed to listen well. Responded like someone who listens. You didn't tell me too many details about your life. You had a rugged handsomeness to you. "Bad Guy" vibes... full head of curly hair... my age? Younger? Much younger... hard to tell... besides, it was dark. We spoke for half an hour or so. I was getting cold, so we walked to the store on the corner of Oswego and Niagara. You bought cigarettes while I bought an ice cream. "I thought you were cold," you said. I was, but I wanted ice cream, a sandwich bar.

I wanted you to feel safe in the community. Already, I wanted to help, introduce you to James Bay. I told you about the Church of Truth. I immediately went into an explanation about it being non-denominational, not wanting to put you off if you weren't the religious type. I rarely think of it the other way around: someone who would enter a church if there were a minister or priest as opposed to not having one. Anyway, I was intrigued by you and the simple spontaneity of it, the aliveness of that moment, and the sincerity I felt in your tone, your honesty, or so it seemed.

I asked for your email so I could stay in touch and perhaps show you around the neighborhood sometime. You said you had a curfew and had to be home by 11, or was it 10? Maybe 11. You offered to walk me further, which was when I started to feel uncomfortable. I insisted I wanted to go the rest of the way on my own, so we said goodbye, and I watched you walk away.

My friend, Linda, lived nearby, just around the corner from me. I went to her place. I told her about you. She said I was nuts to even think about contacting you. "I know you, June (there's that June, not Junie). You are kind and have a big heart and want to 'save' everyone. This guy has been in prison for twenty years. You think you're safe with him? Girl, get a grip!"

It made me mad. I wanted to trust. I wasn't willing to take on the belief that you were going to rape me or kill me with an axe. But I became cautious. And every time I thought of you... and I had your email in my little notebook, I stopped myself from emailing you. I knew if I did, you would then have my email address and my name. Did I tell you my name? Was it June, the hardened one, or Junie, the softer, more trusting one?

I guess I was a bit nervous. I guess I was concerned. Or busy. Or a coward or something else. The bottom line was that when I thought about you, I felt angry with myself. Angry that I offered to keep in touch. It wasn't you who asked for my contact information; I was the one who asked for yours. Old habits die hard, and you were the "Bad Boy." I got your email, but I never wrote. How many times did you get that? A few days out of lock up, and you have a conversation with someone, and they offer to keep in touch, help you to get to know the neighbourhood, and then never call. Ever. Can't trust anyone. Again!

Then, what was it, a few weeks ago? I was with my friend Patricia Zimmer at Serious Coffee on Cook Street, and I saw you. I recognized you. You were with a woman, and I went right up to you and pretended that I wasn't sure who you were. "Are you Kevin?" Of course, I knew who you were. I felt I needed to remind you of who I was. You knew. You remembered me and asked me how the writing was going. Had I told you about my writing? I must have, sharing another piece of myself with a stranger. June or Junie?

I apologized for not calling, telling you how busy I'd been, you know, writing and all. You were gracious and told me not to worry. Not the first time someone had brushed you off upon reflection of who you were or had been. Not to worry. I felt better. I had the chance to tell you that I felt bad about my actions, absolve myself of guilt.

But it didn't stop there. No. It didn't stop. I couldn't get you out of my mind. Fantasied. The intensity of your look. The mystery of you. I wanted to know your life. And I wanted to know who I could be with you, June, or Junie. Why? Why? Why June? Why Junie?

Maybe I saw myself in you in some strange way, a fellow human being trying to remake himself. Or maybe you knew who you were, and it was me who was lost. I walked down to the halfway house where you had been living when we met. Didn't even know if you were still there. You were and I left a message. A few minutes later, you were sitting across from me at the Ogden Point Cafe. It was a short visit... but we met again the next day. We talked about faith.

Why? Why am I interested in a man who has spent the last twenty years in prison for murder?

I told Val. She understood. She wanted me to exercise caution. She wanted me to keep my eyes open. She said people can change, heal... I didn't even know your last name. But you knew mine. Maybe. Did I tell you, or did I leave it at June... or Junie?

The times we saw each other after that were few, but our interactions were friendly, easy, comfortable. Maybe I wasn't attracted to your "Bad Boy" vibe anymore, maybe I had changed. Maybe I have changed and healed.

Thank you, Kevin, for helping me heal June and move into Junie. Now I know people can change and heal, even me.

With Blessings, wherever you are,

Junie

Dear Reader,

There are some friendships that shape the very rhythm of our hearts, even when time and distance pull us apart. Suki was that friend for me. She was my bestest childhood friend and my greatest heartbreak. After decades of silence, life opened the door for us to find each other again, and in that reunion, the grief of my youth transformed into a love that had been waiting patiently to be remembered.

Love,

Junie

Dearest Suki,
    if you only knew...

It has been just over a year since I contacted you on Facebook. Somehow, I summoned up all the courage I had—yes, it still took that, even though forty-three years had passed—and put in a friend request. You can't imagine my surprise and glee at a prayer answered, which was granted in mere seconds. You replied!

Later, you told me you didn't have to think twice. And then just a few months later, you were walking toward me in Darlene's co-op courtyard in Toronto. I couldn't believe that we were both sixty-four! The last time we laid eyes on each other, we were only twenty. It felt like my life ended that dreary, cold, and rainy day in London when you told me you never wanted to see me again. And despite my protestations, you wouldn't hear, you wouldn't listen. Instead, you sent me away, and in that moment, I not only lost you but also the memories that I had treasured since the day we met, when we were only six years old.

And there we were, racing toward one another in that courtyard lined with sunflowers reaching for the sky just as we were reaching for one another's hearts. The first words out of your mouth after our long, loving embrace were, "I will never let go of you again." I melted into those words; I felt I was home again. I had just been welcomed home again.

Today, as I recount this story, we are once again 3,000 miles apart, and don't speak that often; we email even less. The wounds, however, have been healed, and the love is eternal.

No words are adequate to describe how it feels to have you back in my life. Going back to last summer, not only was I blessed to see you, but I was equally blessed to see your father.

Your father was like my second dad. I was probably at your house as much as I was in my own. He was kind and gentle and always gave me the feeling that he loved me as much as he did his own children; I adored him. When I lost you all those years ago, I also lost my chosen family.

You told me he was very, very ill. Your mom had died just months before. So much grief, my heart broke for you. Now, your dad, who had always been your very best friend, was close to dying, and it was such a heartbreaking time for you. It meant the world to me when you told your dad I was coming to see you in Toronto, and that we were reuniting, he told you he wanted to see me too. It couldn't have been more mutual.

When we went to see him at his home, he was waiting for us on the sofa, and the moment I laid eyes on him, I started to weep. I didn't realize until that moment how much I had missed him.

I sat down beside him, and we hugged; his eyes were also filled with tears. It was a breathtaking moment for both of us. We began to talk, and even though he was now in his nineties and in pain, his mind was as sharp as a whip. He insisted on taking us to dinner that night, and despite all the odds, he did. It was truly like old times.

Just two days after I returned to Victoria, he passed away. It's hard not to believe, on some level, he waited for me to come. At least that's the story I want to tell myself.

Oh Suki! I loved our time together in Toronto; we held hands as we walked the streets of our old neighbourhood and reminisced about old times. When we talked about the quarrel that pulled us apart, we both had diametrically opposed memories of it. Isn't it interesting how often we do that? How many times do we hold onto our stories as 'The Truth' when, of course, there could be so many other interpretations. Each of us can occupy the same time and space with the same outer experience, yet it is our inner experience and personal perceptions that will determine its meaning. But we didn't care. It doesn't matter anymore. We're hardly going to try to win sides at this point. That would have been insanity in my books!

My dearest friend has returned to fill me up in ways I had forgotten. I not only feel I have my best friend back, but I have a lifetime of history restored to me. It has been very painful to think of my childhood and teenage years because there were very few memories where you were not a part of them.

And now that chapter has been healed.

I wrote about it, though, in one of my books, *Re-Write Your Life*. It is called "Letting Go."

In it, I call you, Lisa, to keep your identity hidden. Now it is no longer a secret. Lisa was the name you were going to give to a baby girl, had you had one. You could hardly believe I remembered that. We both remembered so much about each other that we had forgotten ourselves.

I promised you I would share the story I wrote about you, about us.

Here it is:

"I never used to think of myself as a rebel, but I suppose in some ways I have been. I did not do what society had expected of me back then. I did not marry out of high school like my sisters did. My best friend and I had spoken for years about traveling together, long before it was popular for girls to do such things. We were barely nineteen, and we did it. We flew to New York from Toronto in the early fall of 1970. Then we walked aboard a student ship that sailed across the Atlantic for ten days to Le Havre, France, and then on to Southampton, England, where we docked, disembarked, and stepped into a future that neither of us could have predicted. We intended to be away for a year. It didn't happen. At least not together.

This was where the biggest letting go of my young life happened and it took me years and endless tears to finally let go of the pain.

Lisa and I met in Grade 2. I don't remember what initially made me follow her around until she finally agreed to be my friend. She did, and we became inseparable. We walked to school together every day, did our homework together at night, and in those long, hot, Toronto summers, we hung out with each other in the park behind the apartment building where we lived. One summer, when

I was twelve, I was sent to Camp Kvutza, and we cried bitter tears in the parting. We wrote to each other every day.

At eighteen, Lisa got engaged, and so did I. Within a year, both of our engagements ended, and we decided to make our childhood dream come true; to set out on a travel adventure. It didn't unfold the way we envisioned it. The following is how I remember it; Lisa remembers it differently. Once aboard the ship, Lisa stopped talking to me. For ten unbearable days, she ignored me. None of my pleading brought her any closer to telling me what was wrong.

In desperation, I pretended to have fun with the new friends I was meeting, but inside, I was consumed by agonizing loneliness. Not until the day we sighted land and were to disembark did Lisa finally let me know what was going on. She was carrying a horrific burden, a dreadful secret that she only felt safe enough to tell me when we got to the other side of the world. (It's her secret, so I'm choosing not to share it.) As she spoke, she wept, and I held her. We wept together. It was beyond what either of us had any experience with or were prepared for. It was totally outside our comfort zone, and neither of us had the tools to know how to handle it.

Within a very short time, it brought about the end of our friendship. I returned home from Europe a year later with my first experience of clinical depression. Many things preceded and contributed to that crisis, but none that held the weight of despair like losing Lisa's love.

Letting go of her was among the hardest things I ever had to do. Somewhere in the letting go process, I wrote this: "She enters my thoughts out of nowhere, and suddenly I'm consumed by that familiar longing again—a crippling emptiness that has all the scars of a motherless child—vainly searching shadowed street corners for the one who's never, ever coming back. I suppose I'll go to my grave with this. Therapy and the years have played their part in helping to dull the ache, but it comes back anyway. It comes back in torrents and floods and then ebbs away again, leaving me like the darkened streets, desolate and bare.

And again someday when I least expect to remember—when I'm doing something menial like ironing a shirt or crossing a street or thinking about buying myself flowers, she'll return in full life-size form and dimensions, equipped with sounds and tastes and smells and the movie projector is running on automatic and we're children again, running in the park and giggling over some silly joke or about one of the teachers at school. The secrets we told each other, all our secrets, and what we shared of all of our dreams for what we wanted when we grew up. We shared it all. Teenage tears, fears, and the excitement over a new boy.

And we sang, how we loved to sing! We knew all the words to every song. Nat King Cole's song 'Smile' was ours. And we did everything together. Best friends. We were best friends. Blood sisters. Didn't we cut our index fingers until they bled when we were eight, then rubbed them together and swore an oath to never, ever part. It worked. She lives inside my veins. It's only in the other world she ceases to exist—the one that shows its face to the others. But the woman-child who lives inside me and peaks out only now and again is the one who remembers, and she's the one who misses you, Lisa. She's the one who wishes more than anything else in this entire life that you would come back and love her again."

It has been two decades since I wrote that, and the pain has long since subsided. I have a flood of loving tenderness when I think of her. Wherever she is, I hope she is happy and fulfilled in her life. As with all experiences, I know they can heal and bring us into a deeper understanding of ourselves and the world around us. I understand that if we had had the tools, we would have surpassed the crisis that separated us forever. For many years, I blamed her for rejecting me, but in truth, I did that to myself. I locked myself into a coffin of guilt and hopelessness, so it was no wonder I became clinically depressed.

Letting go has been much easier of late. I've had the death of both my mother and sister in the past year and a half to help me practice. A spiritual tenet that seems to work for me is to accept what is. To fight against what is only creates suffering and unnecessary drama. I can try to hold on, but in this temporal world, nothing stays the same. It's helpful to remember that I have a conscious choice in how to respond to situations. Do I want peace and contentment, or do I want to suffer? If I want to suffer, I hold on and fight. If I want peace, I can accept what is and see the beauty and perfection in all situations. It doesn't mean I don't feel pain or sadness. I do. And then I embrace it and hold compassion for the part of me that is hurting. In the honouring of the pain, it dissipates, and the letting-go process is organic. I don't make it go away; it just does, and I move into a state of well-being.

When I think back on Lisa today, it's like a very long-ago dream, but one that had a tremendous impact on my life. I learned early about the bitterness of separation and betrayal. I learned of guilt and anguish, and it took years to stop re-enacting the same patterns. Hopefully, I have learned enough to pass on what I have learned in a way that can assist in lessening someone else's pain.

Wherever you are, Lisa, know you are loved. I am grateful for the gift of remembering us all those years ago and acknowledging where I am today. I am at peace. I pray that you are, too."

And now I do know you are at peace, and that we are both at peace with each other. Thank you hardly begins to describe the gratitude I have in my heart for the Universe for reuniting us in the senior years of our lives.

I love you, Suki, with all of my heart.

Your bestest friend,

Junie

Dear Reader,

Whan I think of my childhood, Arny is one of the people who stands out most vividly in my heart. He was a quiet, gentle boy who carried both loneliness and strength, and though I never found the courage to tell him how much he meant to me, his presence shaped me in ways I only later came to understand. This letter is my way of honouring him and the love and friendship that remained unspoken

Love,

Junie

Dearest Arny,
  if you only knew...

I close my eyes, and I am gazing out my window at the park. Earlier, when we first moved to 57 Neptune Drive and I was six, it was an open field with scattered patches of weeds and grass. There were rabbit holes, ant hills, and mice nests. At night, when it was still, you could hear the frogs and crickets. That was until the cranes showed up one day. They tore everything alive out of there to put down manicured lawns with swings and teeter-totters. It was OK, but I had to get used to it. The field was my first taste of freedom, and it's where I remember you the most.

My bedroom window held the perfect vantage point for looking out to see who was there at any given moment. On days when I felt anxious and insecure, looking out at my friends in the park made me feel connected. Even though I wasn't with them, there was something good about knowing they were there.

It was here, Arny, that I often observed you. I felt a kinship with you. We were both eleven years old. Looking now through my young girl's eyes, I see you there. It's raining outside, and you are on the swing going back and forth and back and forth slowly, always slowly. The rain is washing over you, yet you don't seem to notice or care. You've been there an hour already, and I wonder what you are thinking. Why are you not at home, where it's warm and dry? I want to go and get you and bring you inside, but I don't dare. We were both so shy, and I didn't know what to say.

My young heart ached for you. I felt your loneliness in my bones. It lingered there next to my own. Although we never spoke the words, I know somehow, we felt safe with each other. I would look over at you across the aisle from me, sitting at your little brown desk in Miss Stewart's class, drawing pictures.

You drew airplanes and cars. Detailed, precise. Perfect replicas of the models. I could see how beautiful they were. Sometimes Miss Stewart would catch you unaware and shout at you just like she used to do with me when I was daydreaming. I can't remember, did she stomp over to you, grab your beautiful pictures, and crumble them up? Did she rip your heart out as she did mine every time she made me stay after class to tell me how stupid I was? Yes, I can bet that your tender heart was torn apart with the desecration of your quiet renderings. I know mine was. Every time she hurt you, I wept.

At other times, from my bedroom window, I watched you run. You ran the full circumference of the park. You made it into a racetrack, running round and round, picking up speed each time. Sometimes I couldn't even tell if it was you because you were indistinguishable from the trees across the way. But of course, as soon as you stopped, I knew it was you because you would take up residence once again on the swing, gently swaying back and forth, not violently like you're running. Here, you caught your breath after running faster than any imaginary monster in your mind could catch up to. It was just a slow and steady back and forth, back and forth.

Were you able to make them disappear? Did they fly out into the wind as you picked up speed? Who were those monsters, Arny? Who was it that haunted you? You were determined to beat them.

Beyond the park, you won every single track and field race. You became the fastest runner in all the city competitions. You put your mind to something, and you knew how to make it happen. But you never bragged. In fact, you rarely ever spoke.

Do you remember the time when we were in Grade 3 and I chose you to be Peter in the Peter Pan skit, and you tried to say no, but I must have badgered you until you reluctantly said, "Okay." I was Wendy. We had our little scripts. Sometimes, on my way to school, having crossed the creek that led to the path onto Baycrest Avenue, I would spot you up ahead. I would run and catch up and, with hopeful expectancy, ask, "So, Arny, did you memorize your lines yet?"

You wouldn't answer. You just walked in the slow way you did, head down.

"Com'on, Arny, did you?" Did you?" I knew you hadn't, but I wouldn't let up. Eventually, if I didn't stop pestering you, you would shake your head, which seemed to hang down even lower now, and whisper, "Sorry."

Now, being totally insensitive, I would cry out, "But Arny, we've only got two days left. You've got to do it. You've got to!"

I can't remember if you did learn them or not. The memory that stands out for me most is that my mother took me to the hairdresser's the night before the skit. My long, beautiful hair was now a short pixie cut. I could have played your part. I looked more like Peter Pan than you did!

Another time I'm sure I tortured you was when we were nine or ten and I made you write something in my autograph book. This is what you wrote, "Roses are red, violets are green. My face is funny, but yours is a scream."

That was one of the few times you showed a sense of humour, but apparently, I didn't see it that way. I couldn't believe you wrote such a mean thing to me. I was mortified. I wanted you to show me in writing how much you liked me, so I made you write another one. You sighed, but did it anyway.

This time you wrote, "Roses are red, violets are green, my face is funny, but yours is a nice-lookin' sort of face."

Oh, Arny, how it makes me smile to think of you. It also makes me sad to think I picked on you so much. Was that my awkward way of showing you I liked you? You were a gentle boy. And you became a gentle man.

Later, on my sixteenth birthday, I had the shock of my life. The doorbell rang. I opened it only to find a gorilla in front of me that started belting out Happy Birthday with the most amazing voice! Those were the years of singing telegrams. When the song was over, the person with the remarkable voice removed his gorilla head, and it was none other than you! You, the boy who was so shy. How was this possible? And more than that, I never knew you could sing! Yet I did know that you pushed the edges. Maybe more than most people. Life challenged you, and you challenged it back, and you won. You always seemed to win... at least on the outside. I often wondered what was going on inside. Had you ever known happiness?

Many years later, I was attending a wedding. When I went up to dance, I looked up at the stage and there you were at the microphone, so handsome in your tuxedo, engaging the guests with your warmth. You were not only the MC, but you were also the leader of the band. Your band! The Arny Wiskin Band. My heart swelled with happiness for you. As time went on, yours became the most sought-after wedding and Bar Mitzvah band in Toronto.

Who would have ever guessed that the little boy who was too shy to learn lines for a skit, drew cars and airplanes to tune out the teachers, sat alone swinging back and forth for hours in the rain, would become a world-class athlete and performer? But you did.

I remember running into you years later. We went for a coffee. You seemed quiet and shy again. We both were. I felt I hardly knew you, and in another way, I felt as though I was inside your skin. Just like it felt when I would watch you from my bedroom window all those years ago. So familiar and yet so distant at the same time.

It was awkward being with you again as an adult, our youth long gone. I had no words to bridge the gap. I thought about other men I had known. The Bad Boys. The ones I seemed to attract back then. And worse, fell for only to have my heart broken over and over.

I realized then that I had loved you. But I was too young and too scared to know what to say or to know how to be with a man such as you. A man so pure of heart.

My friend Kelly called me tonight, and I shared your story with her. She said, "Hey, why don't you find Arny on Facebook or Google and establish contact again?"

I couldn't believe I hadn't thought of that. I got so excited to learn where you were and be in contact again. After a long search, in utter shock, I found your obituary.

"WISKIN, Arny—Passed away peacefully
on July 6, 2009, at home.

They mentioned family members, so I knew it was you, and this news so saddens me. Devastated, if you want to know the truth. How I wished I could have told you what was in my heart long ago. While you were still alive.

So, dearest Arny, this story is a small token of my love. My heart would be overjoyed to know that wherever you are, you are still singing.

God bless you, Arny, wherever you are.

Junie

Dear Reader,

You are in for a treat! This letter is written to the summer camp that gave me my first true taste of joy and belonging. At a time when home life felt heavy, Camp Kvutza opened my heart to happiness, friendship, and sacred connection. It was a place where I learned that love, kindness, and togetherness could be the foundation for life itself. I share with you my experiences as a young girl taken by surprise by a slightly rundown camp that opened me to my deepest spiritual awakening of my life. The magnitude of that experience shaped the rest of my life, which, from the perspective of an eleven-year-old, was nothing less than miraculous.

Love,

Junie

Dearest Camp Kvutza,
  if you only knew...

When I think about my favourite summer as a kid, it is you I think of. There was never any question. You gave me the most beautiful experience I could have ever asked for, as you unwittingly opened my eyes and heart to what's possible when there is unity, love, creativity, cooperation, joy, music, discussion, play, and kindness.

I wonder if certain locations on the map of the world have soul contracts just like humans do; that before people inhabit them, they are destined for greatness. Did you know that you were destined to hold the hearts of thousands of children over three decades and offer them a foundation of values that would sustain them for a lifetime? At least that's how I saw it. And that's the reputation that you had. To have gone to Camp Kvutza made you an alumnus of some privileged status or to have belonged to a secret club. Not privileged by economic class, that's for sure, but by nobility.

I remember gathering in the parking lot at the Bialik Hebrew Day School on Bathurst St., along with bunches of other kids, ready to board a bus to take us to you. You were located on the northeastern shores of Lake Erie near Dunville, Ontario, an almost three-hour drive filled with anticipation for the weeks to come.

I was being sent to you for the entire month of July, leaving behind my best friend Suki. How could I bear it? And I didn't know a single other person on the bus. But I did know that to be going to you was a privilege, and not an easy thing for my family to afford.

I remember crying at the thought of being away from Suki for a whole month. Or being away from home at all for that long. But once I arrived, well, I entered a life that I simply didn't want to leave.

You, Camp Kvutza, became heaven on earth. Not only was being with you a break from the troubles at home, but it was a blessing to my soul. I became happy. I didn't know what happiness meant before that. Not really. Yes, for short periods of time, I guess. But I simply woke up happy every day with you because the counsellors and the rest of the staff seemed to have a key to knowing how to do just that, being happy. There was so much kindness and enthusiasm, and they planned awesome activities— well, I just fit in, I guess. I opened up to being with you, and you opened up to me.

The cabins were kind of run down, and the grounds were rugged and raw, but to me, you were sacred ground. Everything about you was somehow sacred, even though I wouldn't have called it that at the time, not having the vocabulary. But in retrospect, sacred is precisely how it feels.

My age group got to sleep in tents, which notoriously blew down whenever there was a strong wind. It wasn't uncommon to return from an activity to find our tent on the ground and all our belongings strewn about. The next half hour would be spent giggling as we tried to figure out whose things belonged to whom! There was no guessing when it came to the pink rollers that I got teased mercilessly for. I dutifully put them in my hair every night just as I had watched my older sisters do before they left home to get married. So, what if this was camp? A girl still had to look pretty, didn't she?

Yes, you were special. Even though there was no boating, water skiing, or horseback riding like some of the other camps my friends went to, there was more spirit and togetherness than I had ever known.

My camp counsellors were fun and kind, and I quickly made friends with the girls in my tent. I became known as the fastest runner in all the relay races and the best pitcher in the softball league. ˙

At night, after the evening activity, the entire camp gathered around the flagpole to lower the flag, holding hands under the stars, singing Ha-Tichvah, the Hebrew National Anthem, and "Lylah, Lylah," which is "Taps" in Hebrew, the traditional song for when the national flag of Israel is raised.

There was something about that ritual that aroused a yearning in me for group togetherness that has stayed with me my entire life. It was a sacred ceremony. We were all joined under the stars and under God for a common purpose, to be united and to love each other. No one ever said it, but I knew it in my bones.

From that time forward, I knew there was more to life than what we could see or touch, and I knew this sacredness every time I was in nature or felt love or experienced or witnessed a kind act. And that summer I experienced lots of them.

I felt love from everyone, and I gave freely from my heart. Every day was full and better than the one before. The day that I had to go home on the bus and say good-bye to my new friends, I thought my heart would break beyond repair.

My counsellor, Bella, tried calling my parents to see if there was any chance of my staying with you, Camp Kvutza, for the second month. We all wanted it so badly. But it wasn't possible. I think Dad had already scraped together what little savings he had, or more likely, he went into debt to let me have even one month of summer camp with you. I felt ashamed for being greedy. I also felt angry that I had to leave you. I was the only one who had to go home after only one month. My cabinmates wrote me a song and sang it to me the night before I had to leave. It was sung to the tune of "Moon River," and we all cried.

I stepped onto that bus with tears streaming down my face and cried all the way home. How would I live without you and all of my new friends and memories? Mom met me at that same parking lot with hugs and kisses and apologies that I couldn't stay longer.

As usual, Dad was nowhere to be seen. I figured he was at work, so I didn't even question it. On the drive home, Mom chit-chatted about my sisters, my brother, my nieces and nephews, and general gossip about home. She didn't even mention Dad until we walked in the door. Then she sat me down and said she had something to tell me. My heart sank.

Somehow, I knew...

"Where's Dad? Why haven't you told me about Dad?"

Then, in the gentlest way possible, and fighting back tears, she told me he had a heart attack and was in intensive care at Doctors' Hospital. "But he'll be fine," she uttered, trying to smile and to reassure me. My world collapsed. Here was Dad lying in intensive care, and for the past few hours, all I could think about was how mean he was for not letting me stay with you. I felt so much guilt.

The month of August was spent visiting dad, saying lots of prayers, reuniting with Suki, spending time with my sisters' kids, and writing my friends who got to stay with you. Soon, September came, and little by little, Dad's strength returned. He came home from the hospital and eventually went back to work. I was excited to start my first year at Junior High and felt even more solid having had a summer so filled with love and connection.

Thank you, Camp Kvutza, for gracing me with memories that bring joy to my heart when there were so few that did, back then.

With love and gratitude,

Junie

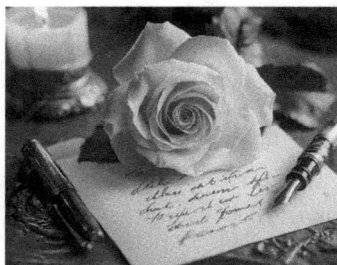

Dear Reader,

In this deeply poignant healing story, we learn how an old woman, an elder, could change the direction of a much younger woman's life. Some people arrive in our lives like a quiet, steady flame, warming us when the world is cold and frightening. Annie was that flame for me, sitting beside me when I had no voice, no strength, and no way to protect myself. She did not ask for anything in return; she simply was a presence that changed the course of my life. This letter is my attempt to reach across time and memory, to honor her, to remember her, and to tell the story of the comfort she gave me when I needed it most.

Love,

Junie

Dearest Annie,
    if you only knew...

I am looking out my window, where I am a writer in residence in Lake Cowichan, BC. It is a rainy, cold day in early January. I came here to finish my book of healing letters, and the next story just has to be yours.

I knew it last night as I looked through the list of letters still to write, and yours popped up at me, and it's as if there is no other. So, I took you on my walk with me earlier, and you were vividly living beside me just as you were in 1974 at the Clarke Institute in Toronto.

We were both patients inside this enormous institution on College Street, but I never understood why you were there. Me? I was definitely not well. You? Every day you occupied yourself in the common room by reading the Toronto Star, Toronto Telegram, and Jerusalem Post. Not one paper. Three! You read the articles out loud, peppered with your astute and insightful commentary, always drawing a group of other interested patients who gathered around you, holding onto your every word!

Me? I'd try to hide. I had nothing to offer or contribute. I had nothing to say about anything. Instead, I hid in my room. The nurses would find me and bring me back to the common room. I'd go back to my room again, and they'd find me again. They wouldn't let me stay in my room. Whenever they brought me back to the common room, I looked for a place where I could sit by myself as far away as possible from everyone else. Yet that never deterred you from walking over, all your papers in hand, to sit in the empty seat beside me. You never asked anything of me. You just sat beside me. Day after day.

My official diagnosis was catatonia. I could sit for hours, staring at a wall, completely frozen. When I had to go to the bathroom, it felt like trying to solve a puzzle with missing pieces. I had to remember how to uncross my legs, figure out which foot to move first, steady myself with a hand on the chair, and somehow get my body to stand up and move. It wasn't walking—it was dragging myself through thick fog. Every step took everything I had. And sometimes, I couldn't do it in time. I'd wet myself trying to remember how to walk. It was humiliating. And terrifying.

Before my parents admitted me to the Clarke Institute, I was at the Branson Hospital on Finch Avenue for a full month. At the end of the month, the head psychiatrist told my parents that there was nothing they could do for me. He told them I must have used a lot of drugs while I was in Europe, and there was no telling if I would ever come out of it. I may have ruined my brain cells forever. He added that they could take me home. I knew he was lying because I hadn't done any drugs, but I didn't have the ability to speak. But I could hear everything, and I remember never being so happy because I could go home. I could go home! That felt so good to me. And I was terrified. I had just been given a living death sentence: that I would be this way forever.

My parents didn't accept that doctor's prognosis. They drove me to the Clarke Institute instead. Oh, Annie, I wanted to die while I was there. I wanted to die so much. I kept wondering why you wanted to sit beside me. I had nothing to say to you. I had nothing to contribute to the conversations that evolved from the current events you read to us each day. Nothing, ever. Why did you do it? Why did you sit beside me? Did you know that it gave me comfort? It did, you know.

Were you in your 90s? You looked like you were. Maybe just your 70s or 80s, but I was in my 20s, so you looked ancient to me. You looked like my Boobbie, and she was very old. Now, I'm seventy-five and I'm sure I look ancient to people in their 20s too. Anyway, Annie, I don't know if you knew that you were the catalyst that brought about my eventual healing.

I was walking past the nursing station one day, and you were there and screaming out of control. What?!!!! I was in shock! I had never seen you like that. The only way I ever saw you was dignified, articulate, calm, and centred. What was going on? I didn't "think" about wanting to come to your defense. I just started screaming, too. The first sounds to come out of me in months!

"What are you doing to Annie?! What are you doing to Annie?!"

I couldn't stop screaming. I was so scared for you! They dragged me away from the nurses' station, and tried to settle me down, but I was "Unsettle-down-able". I wanted to know. I wanted to protect you. I wanted to put my arms around you and then take your hand and the two of us, run like hell out of that place.

I never saw you again after that, Annie. Or maybe I did. To be honest, I don't remember. I may have blocked it out because it was too devastating. Maybe they gave you shock treatment and lined you up to go into that room of horrors, where you would come out an hour later looking like a zombie. Anyway, that may have been the case. Maybe they put you on a different floor. After all, the entire hospital was for people with a mental illness, not just a ward in a wing. We were all identified as 'crazies' in that place.

Or maybe you got discharged. I don't know. All I know is that it stopped feeling safe for me there. I didn't know it felt safe at all until you weren't there sitting beside me anymore. You added a level of comfort that was now gone. But that incident with you screaming in the hall started me on my lifelong healing journey.

Screaming out loud with real words, not just hysteria, thinking someone was hurting you and wanting them to stop, was the beginning of me learning to speak again. Afterwards, when I was in group therapy sessions, I had a voice, I had an opinion, I was able to speak, shyly, bashfully, softly, hesitantly, no confidence or conviction really, but it was a start. And over time, I moved out of being catatonic to being able to speak in full sentences and once again have conversations.

It was a long time later when I heard what happened to you. Apparently, your son, who had Power of Attorney over your house, sold it. Your house in Kensington Market was an enviable place to live. Anyone who knew Toronto back in the day would know that Kensington Market was a happening place. It's where people came to shop in the Spadina/College area. There were several streets filled with bakeries, butcher shops, ethnic cheese shops, fresh vegetables, clothing, coffee shops, music shops: a bit of everything. It was loud and fun and filled with immigrant shopkeepers and shoppers: Jewish, Portuguese, Greek, Italian, Spanish, Jamaicans, you name it!

I can only imagine how horrible that must have been for you, Annie. To have your home taken away from you, right under your nose, by your very own son. I'm so sorry that happened to you. I wish I could have protected you.

I wish I'd had a chance to tell you how you comforted me when I was desperately afraid of life. I pray that you somehow found peace in your remaining years, Annie. I pray that you did.

I will always remember you, and I will always love you.

Love,

Junie

Dear Reader,

Some letters are written to people, some to memories, some even to forces we cannot see. This one is to Death itself—a presence that has lingered close to me for decades, shaping, frightening, and teaching me. Through my own experiences with bipolar illness and suicide attempts, I have come to understand life and death in ways that are raw, intimate, and unflinchingly real. This letter is my attempt to speak openly, to bear witness, and to honor the fragile, precious gift of being alive.

Love,

Junie

Dearest Death,
  if only you knew...

I can't imagine one person who has heard about Robin Williams' death who hasn't been shocked and devastated. I am one of them. I have taken it hard.

As you know, Death, I live with bipolar illness. I was diagnosed when I was twenty. I 'came out' when I was fifty. It was too freakin' scary to do it before then. It was terrifying even then. After all, I had a private psychotherapy practice, worked as a mental health worker in a group home, and gave educational talks in corporations about mental health in the workplace, sponsored by the Canadian Mental Health Association. How could I "come out of the closet" and expect my career to survive? How could I expect to survive?

I had just come out of a hospital after another clinical depression. The phones were ringing. People wanted to come to my new workshops. I couldn't do it. I couldn't lie any more. I couldn't go back to pretending all was well with me when I had spent the last month in a psych ward.

Instead, I wrote *Madness, Masks and Miracles*, a play about the dark night of the soul that everyone on earth experiences at least once in their lifetime. I wrote about the masks we wear to disguise the pain. Who would ever have known of the unspeakable burden that Robin Williams was carrying? Did you, Death? Many of us have learned to have a public facade that can fool the masses. And finally, my play was about the miracles that allow us to take off our masks and be who we really are.

I am one of the lucky ones. I count my blessings. I have had numerous suicide attempts, as you well know. I can't describe to you or anyone what I have come to call the torture chamber of the mind. Well, maybe you do know. Thank God, for the past few years, I have been well, really well.

I've had my moments of unrest, sadness, and overwhelm over the last few years, but I have never even come close to having suicidal thoughts. I don't believe I ever will again. My last attempt led me to a near-death experience, and I woke up in a state of grace, and I have never looked back. Did your grasp slip again, Death?

I am inspired right now to tell this story. A story I have never told in public. The people close to me know it. I have always been too ashamed to tell it. Me, the one who 'came out of the closet' all those years ago, standing on stage at the Vancouver Conference Centre in front of 400 doctors and mental health workers at the International World Assembly for Mental Health, a convention that happened to be in Vancouver when we just started staging the play. They had heard about the play and asked us to perform it for them. It was the worst experience I have ever had. It was also the best experience as it allowed me to speak my truth despite the terror of being criticized, ostracized, marginalized, and hospitalized, yet again.

It feels like light years ago when I 'woke up' in what I can only describe as a state of grace. But the story that preceded it was not pretty. Few people know about it. Today, I came to the computer to do something else. Instead, my fingers are flying off the keyboard telling this story, the one I was always too ashamed to tell.

Bipolar illness has many shapes and sizes. It is not a cookie-cutter disease as some people may think. Oh, look, she's really depressed. Oh look, she's wildly out of control. There are so many layers. Oh, so many! And the sufferers of these illnesses and their family, friends, and caregivers suffer right along with them.

When I was a young girl, and up until recently, NO-ONE spoke about their mental illness, especially in public. The stigma and shame were so unbearably powerful that no one dared to speak up. Hey, I didn't dare until I was fifty! Today, and for several years now, public figures are talking freely about their diagnosis, their pain, and suffering. It's talked about more in the media now than ever, at least here in North America. Still, there is a long way to go.

And it is people who do speak out that make it safe for others to do the same.

But what does all of this have to do with you, Death? After all, you only show up after the trigger has been pulled, the noose tightened, or the pills swallowed. But, then again, perhaps you are present in the days and weeks leading up to a suicide, waiting to pick up the pieces of a shattered soul on the other side.

This is why I speak up: to keep you at bay a little longer so a life can maybe be well lived.

I have been speaking out for a long time now. It doesn't mean I am comfortable about it. The fear of being judged is always there. Even a couple of weeks ago, I posted something on Facebook that referred to my mental health challenges. I got absolutely no response. A few days earlier, I wrote a funny story about getting married, and I got upwards of eighty likes and comments. Yet there were no comments when I mentioned my illness. I felt judged and ashamed, and removed it from Facebook. I understand now that Facebook shows more of people's stories which are funny, uplifting, or engaging, and that perhaps my community didn't see my post. Still, even that speaks volumes about what we choose to ignore in society.

And here I am again coming out even more. Admitting my suicide attempts. Am I crazy to do this? Apparently, I am crazy. Or am I not crazy? Am I wise or am I just a person who knows only too well the dangers of secrets, denial, self-loathing, and hiding in shame? Whatever I may be, all I know is that my fingers are flying off the keyboard, and I know I am not manic. I am being propelled by an inner voice, an energy that says, "There is nothing to hide, Junie. You didn't do anything wrong." Funny how often I still think that I have.

In 2009, I was rushed by ambulance to the Royal Jubilee Hospital in Victoria, British Columbia, with hardly a pulse. I swallowed over 100 prescribed pills. I did not intend to come back. I needed to get out of the torture chamber of my mind, a relentless diatribe in my brain, obsessive, cruel, heart-crushing thoughts of guilt and suicidal ideation, and a body riddled with anxiety and a foreboding that never went away. Month after month after month after month, and I couldn't bear it any longer.

I swallowed 100 pills. It was terrifying. I didn't want to die. I love life, as strange as that may seem. I just wanted out of this body, this mind, this pain that wouldn't go away, something that no one could see because I have honed the disguise so well. An invisible disability. I could even go to work. I could interact with people in a way that no one would have guessed I was suffering. But I knew, and I knew I could not hide it any longer.

So, I wrote letters to the people I loved, gulping down tears, and then emptied out dozens of vials filled with prescription drugs, and I swallowed them all. I was sobbing so loud I was sure neighbours could hear me, but I couldn't stop. I apologized to God and to every family member, to the friends who loved me, to the clients who depended on me, to my pets, to the world. But not to you, Death. You, I knew, I would see soon enough. And I did it anyway. Once again, as in earlier attempts, I called no one. I didn't call an emergency line. I just wanted out, and I didn't believe anyone could help me, except for you. I had lost every ounce of hope that I would ever be able to be well again.

A neighbour who knew I was depressed and had my keys to feed my budgies when I went away, checked in on me. I was told she found me on the floor in the kitchen, where I had swallowed the pills. She called the ambulance. I was rushed to the hospital, but I was already in a coma, which lingered for three days and nights.

Were you disappointed, or are your relieved when a suicide doesn't make it into your arms?

Miraculously, on the fourth day, I opened my eyes and started talking. I felt better than I could ever remember feeling before. The doctors were stunned. Not only were they convinced I would not survive, but they were also certain that if I did, I would have irreparable brain and organ damage. I had neither. Physically, I was well. Mentally, I was what I can only call "in a state of grace." They removed all the tubes and wires from my body and transferred me to the Eric Martin Pavilion, the psychiatric hospital in Victoria. To me it was an ashram.

No, I did not think I was Jesus, going from person to person blessing everyone. I was simply seeing the dozens of men and women in that big room, all beautiful souls, suffering, lost, and in turmoil, just like I had been before I 'woke up." I had nothing but compassion for them and for the staff. I could see their frustration and their own suffering and how they were trying so hard to do their best. During this time of observation, I felt grounded, centered, and at peace in a way I never had before.

Two days after coming out of the coma, I asked a friend to bring me my computer. I knew it was time to write my book. How was that possible? For the past six months or longer, I couldn't even string a sentence together. Even writing an email caused unbearable anxiety. And for me, usually it is writing that save my life. Writing brings me to the other side of my suffering, where the light gets in. And I've been teaching this to others for about twenty years! Before my suicide attempt, that was virtually impossible. There were no words. There was no light.

Now, something inside of me said, "*You must have your computer.*" Maybe it was you, cheering from the sidelines of the veil. Were you my cheerleader then?

A friend brought it to me, and within nine months, my book, *Re-Write Your Life: A Transformational Guide to Writing and Healing the Stories of Our Lives*, was completed and published.

From not being able to write, my words were flowing out of me with passion, and I was loving every moment of it. Why passion? Because I knew, only too well, from both sides of the couch, that it is only in rewriting our painful stories that we find peace. That hanging onto the past in shame and blame and resentments, grief, sorrow, and unforgiveness, will never lead to happiness. It only keeps us stuck. Paralyzed. Grandiose. Depressed. Needing to be right at any cost. It keeps us anywhere but in our hearts.

I knew beyond any doubt, having almost died, that life is precious... oh so precious. And it is not a dress rehearsal. It's real. The years go by. We grow older. One day, we will die and possibly go willingly with you to the other side. But, my God, if I could help even one person find a way to live life in peace and joy and to let go of the past and celebrate their life journey, then nothing was going to stop me. I was going to write and publish that book. I knew this was the most important work I had done up until that time. I had rewritten many of my stories already. Now, from this blessed state, I wrote with an inner conviction of truth that would free not only me, but also others who were drawn to its message.

I still live by it. Yet even now, in this very moment, as I sit in front of this computer, the conviction of speaking my truth out loud is still there, but so is the fear of being judged. I'm not sure if that will ever go away. But how could I even think of that stopping me? I am alive. Robin Williams is not. Nor are countless millions of others across our planet who have ended their lives, and possibly as many still who are on the brink as I write this. I do not envy you your job.

So how can I not speak up? How can we not? Together, as one human family, speak up and out, hold each other's hands, stop judging, and find our way back to our tender hearts. Robin Williams, a brilliant, beautiful, courageous man who brought joy and laughter into the lives of millions of people is dead. Death by suicide. Too young, too soon. Do you grieve, or is this just another day at the office for you?

I happened to be at a movie on Monday, ironically held at Eric Martin, the mental hospital where I had been hospitalized, where they have movie nights and the like open to the public. I was there to watch the documentary, *Of Two Minds*, which was riveting. A stunning depiction of several people living with bipolar illness. It was sad, funny in parts, and oh so very, very real. But then my friend, whom I was saving a seat for, sat down and told me the news about Robin Williams. I had to leave the theatre and go to the bathroom because I started to cry. Once I was in the bathroom, in a lone cubicle, I allowed myself to sob.

In the most sad and ironic way, it is in his death that I am given the courage to come out once again, to come out of the closet about my own attempted suicides. I am hoping that, in doing so, I will be able to let go of some of my guilt and shame. I am doing my best to reach into my heart and offer myself compassion for the states of terror and hopelessness that drove me to want to end my life. To reassure myself that I didn't do anything to cause pain and suffering to others purposely. If I or anyone else who is at that critical place could make a rational choice to do it differently, to find a magical cure to be well again and not hurt themselves or the people who love them and they love too, oh, if only. If only.

Since the last attempt, I have been living in deep gratitude and deep humility. There isn't a day that goes by that I do not remember to thank God. Why me? Why was my life spared and not Robin Williams? Not countless others? I don't know. I only know I am here. And I am here to make a difference in whatever ways I can. And one of the ways, I sense, is in writing this and sharing it here with you. And tomorrow and the day after that, it will hopefully be with words and deeds of kindness for whoever shows up on my path.

And that's what we can all do. We can't all be writers or social activists on the front lines. But we can offer gifts of kindness first to ourselves, nurture ourselves into healthy minds and bodies, and spread the kindness to every living being we meet.

Thank you, Death, for not taking my hand each time I tried to come to you years ago. Thank you for being patient with me as I stumbled through my life, trying to find my footing. Thank you, Death, for helping me see how important my life is.

... and with love to Robin Williams, wherever he may be,

Love,

Junie

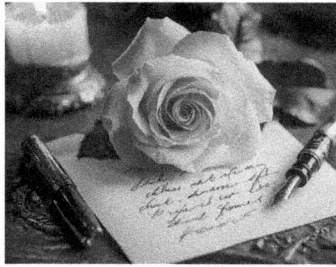

Dear Reader,

This is a letter to an illness so devastating that receiving the diagnosis can stop one in their tracks. It's a diagnosis that affects everyone, not only the person who is ill. I wrote this letter to my first cancer—a presence I both feared and found mysterious, a teacher in ways that were painful, humbling, and unavoidable. In the midst of diagnosis, grief, and uncertainty, this letter is my attempt to speak my truth, to bear witness to fear, sorrow, and resilience. It is a prayer, a plea, and a declaration of the life I still want to live.

Love,

Junie

Dearest Cancer,
     if you only knew...

You frighten me. I don't know what to make of you. Why did you come? What do you have to tell me? Is my time on earth limited? I sometimes wonder how a person can experience this amount of pain and still live. But I want to live. I want to know what I can do to get better. I have employed every modality I know. I have been eating only the healthiest of foods, recommended by homeopaths, naturopaths, and nutritionists. I meditate, I pray, I listen to affirmations, and I journal my thoughts, feelings, hopes, dreams, regrets, sadness, anger, and fear. And now, I am writing to you, dear Cancer. You have inhabited an area of my body and now seem to want to move beyond it into other areas, flooding new cells with your disease. I am scared... and yet mysteriously, at the same time, I am not.

This year, you have taken away so many of my friends. Some weren't even sick until you showed up, and within hardly any time at all, such as in the case of my beautiful friend, Teya; she took her last breath only three months after you invaded her body.

My dear friend Pat and I would sometimes bump into each other at the cancer clinic, not knowing we had treatments on the same day. Her healthy husband, Allan, who was taking care of her, got sick himself. He was taken to the hospital with severe stomach pains and died within a couple of days. She had to go on alone. Well, she was not entirely alone; her two beautiful sons and their wives were there for her every day, as were so many friends who loved her. But her husband was gone. And now she's gone too. It's almost too much to bear.

My husband, David, is here, but not here. I don't think he can handle it very well, so he stays away or in another room. I ache for his touch, and sometimes I drag myself out of bed and ask him to please come into the bedroom and just hold me or talk to me or read to me or... And he does... but leaves as soon as he thinks I am asleep. Occasionally, he'll come to bed. On Thursdays, he goes to The Spiral Café to play music with his buddies, and I encourage him to do so as it's medicine for his soul. When he comes home, he says hello, tells me about the great music played that night, and passes on love from our musician friends. Then he retires to the living room. I think seeing me this way is almost impossible for him to bear after losing his only and beloved daughter, Cat, ten years ago. My heart aches for him. I feel he is all locked up inside, and I can't seem to reach him. If only he would open up and talk to me. I can be there for him, too. I'm still me inside this skeletal 90-pound body. It would bring us closer.

Sometimes, like now, I feel lonely, empty, and lost. Thank God for my friends who come by and help out or just sit with me. Their presence is enough. We don't have to say a word. It's all there permeating the silence... the love, the caring, the concern, the genuine heart and soul connection. And I'm also grateful for the drugs that take away the pain for a while and help me sleep so I don't have to think. Last week, Dr. Sherman suggested that the palliative care team come and assess me. That doesn't sound too good. OK, enough complaining.

I've asked you to show me everything I haven't dealt with, things I have been afraid to look at, things that are unconscious but living in my cells, nevertheless, situations, events, beliefs, paradigms, whatever they are, no matter how hideous, show them to me, bring them into the light of my consciousness so I can work with my therapists and do whatever I need to on my own to heal and put closure on them.

Some memories have been unbearable, but it's OK... because I need to heal everything. But listen, God, can I not just set an intention from my heart and soul to heal everything that needs healing, you know, in one fell swoop? I'm willing to forgive everyone and everything I've been unwilling to forgive before, although I will not condone cruel behaviour. I'm still willing to see everyone innocent at their core on a spiritual level. Or perhaps right now it's not so much about that, but rather, it's about speaking up and not worrying so much about what people think.

I'm feeling weary now, God. Bottom line, I want to live. Can you please just sweep me with a clean bill of health and let me go back into my life where I can continue to be a healer, teacher, mentor, and friend? Did you know that I've already started my next book, *Escalating Bliss, Inspired by Cancer*?

While lying here, I have thought of all the stories I've never dared to tell Maybe this is my opportunity to finally have a voice I've kept silent all these years. Oh, and I've almost completed, *If You Only Knew: A Book of Healing Letters*. I want to live to see these books in print. I want to live to feel the sunshine on my face again. I want to live to know that my life still matters. Please, God, let me live, and be a blessing upon this earth.

Love,

Junie

Dear Reader,

Sometimes, people appear in our lives exactly when we need them most, though we may not realize it at the time. They arrive as teachers, mentors, or angels, helping us navigate challenges we could never face alone. This letter is to one such person in my life, Roger, whose kindness, guidance, and unwavering belief in me shaped some of my most pivotal moments. Without him, I might not have had the courage to create my play, *Madness, Masks & Miracles*. I want to share his story with you and the profound impact one human heart can have on another.

Love,

Junie

Dearest Roger,
   if you only knew...

I have come to believe that we make contracts with people while we are on the other side, to meet up on earth at a particular time and place to play a role in each other's lives. Of course, we forget that we made such contracts, or there would be no surprises—things we delight in once they arrive, or oh, no... how do I run from this before it makes its appearance!? Both are gifts. The angels of mercy and kindness, and those who teach us the hardest lessons. You, dear Roger, came to me as an angel of mercy and kindness and continue to be to this very day. It had been many years since we had been in touch when you suddenly showed up at the Music Benefit Party that was being held for me by David's musician friends to help me navigate my way through cancer financially.

There you were, standing larger than life—a mock hallucination? I thought it must be because I searched for you after it was over, and you were nowhere to be found. You left without a trace... other than a mystery man who left a ridiculously large amount of money in cash, and no one knew it was you. Of course, it wouldn't have even occurred to me that it might be you because I wasn't sure I even saw you for real, and even if I had, I wouldn't know you would leave a crazy sum of money like that! And when I did find out it was you, you told me that you just stepped off a plane from Asia—a gazillion-hour flight and took yourself right to the door of The McTavish Academy, having read about it on Facebook. What?! You cared about me that much!? Wow!

I am so grateful you followed up the next day and solved the mystery as to whether I fantasized you or not. Nope, I did not! You were in Victoria, and later that day, you appeared in the flesh at our home. I was even graced with yet another visit before you had to leave for good. These will always be treasured memories.

During the first visit, you once again gifted me with money—an outrageously generous sum. Even as I type this, I have tears of humility and gratitude. You asked for nothing in return. You gave it to me simply out of the kindness of your heart. You obviously cared about me still, even after all those years, decades, apart, with hardly any communication at all.

The first time we met was when you were assigned to be my social worker after I left the mental health ward at St. Paul's Hospital. I think that is where I was. I've been in others since then, and before that, so I am honestly not sure. My stays in mental wards are a blur in my brain.

My young life was a revolving door in and out of mental institutions after being diagnosed with manic-depressive illness when I was only twenty. I bravely moved beyond it, though, didn't I? I decided not to make mental illness my identity and have worked very hard over the years to be sure of that. Unfortunately, the illness has a tricky way of seducing you back into its unpredictable forcefield just when you think you are out of the woods. So, I've learned to make use of the tools I have cultivated in order to stay healthy and resilient, non-negotiable! And my whole career has been teaching others to do the same. This past year and a half, however, has surely tested those skills to the limit. But I digress!

So, there you were, welcoming me into your office. Your open and warm smile helped to put me at ease right away. Kindness oozed out of your every pore. You had a cool ponytail and were young and handsome to boot! I felt you were someone I could trust—that being a social worker wasn't just your occupation; it was your heart's work.

Over time, you helped me dissolve my shame and embarrassment for coming out of a mental ward, for being on social assistance, and for needing your help at all. After all, I was a psychotherapist with a background of successfully helping others, so how the hell did I end up here again?

Well, I did, and in time, I began standing taller because you were treating me like a whole person, not a broken one.

In one of our meetings, I said, "One day, Rog, I'm going to write a play about my experiences and the stigmas associated with mental illness." You didn't reply by saying, "Let's not get ahead of ourselves." No, you said, "I'll be in the audience, front row centre." You may have been thinking, *Poor girl, she's still delusional,* but I doubt it. Or perhaps you could see something in me that made it possible to imagine it with me. Whatever you were thinking, you did nothing but make me feel that I could find the ways to make it happen.

There have been pivotal times in my life when someone's "seeing me" has been the catalyst to help me believe in myself. You were the catalyst, then. That one remark from your heart to mine carried the gold that propelled me to co-write the script, find the actors, and everything else that was needed to get that play staged. No words could ever thank you enough for being the wind beneath my wings, Roger Greenberg!

I hope you have known such grace in your life, too. That earth angels and celestial angels appear seemingly out of nowhere and hold you when you are in need of being held. May you always know there is an angel by your side.

A year or so after sharing that dream with you, it became a reality. The play was written. We acted it out with the scripts still in our hands at a "reading" for a small number of people.

True to your word, there you were in the audience. Well, almost true to your word. You were not front row and centre. You never seem to position yourself there. Was it the back row? I'm not sure, but there you were, humbly sitting in the background, not wishing to stand out or draw attention to yourself. But I saw you there, and it lit up my heart to know you had come.

After it was over, we put out a request to the audience for volunteers to help us take the play further. There were sign-up sheets in the program. Later, when I went home and read if anyone signed up, OMG—not only did you agree to volunteer, you put your name down as Stage Manager. What?!! Seriously! And, well, you know the rest.

Producing that play was not easy by a long shot! Yet you showed up every step of the way and beyond the call of duty. Duty? What duty! No one was paying you. You were volunteering your precious time and energy because you believed in the message and because you believed in me. Roger, you will always remain as one of my greatest teachers, mentors, and friends for your unconditional acts of kindness and love.

I could have written another play called *Behind the Scenes Madness* to illustrate what transpired during production. It was beyond crazy, yet in spite of the drama and insanity which you witnessed, not from afar, but this time, front and centre, holding me steady every time there was a major crisis—from directors leaving, to the play being cancelled by the World Assembly for Mental Health just days before our opening night and on and on it went.

And you know what, even though producing that play brought me to my knees in desperation more than once, it was so worth it. I knew it in my heart from conception. We never really know when we say something kind to someone or do something like produce a play that touches others or simply offer a smile to a stranger, how it will impact their life... and then add to that the ripple effect. To this day, I still receiving positive feedback from people who watched the video of the play, and it propels them onto a healing path they had not known was possible beforehand.

And the play did go on! The professional communities widely acclaimed it, but then my life took a different spin. When the play was over, I sank into a deep depression. Lee took off to Korea to teach English. He told me he wanted to go somewhere where, "Mental illness was not part of the vocabulary!" Good luck!

Anyway, Roger, you lifted me up, time and time again, before the play began, during, and after, and to this very day.

You have the ability to not only listen, but truly hear and respond lovingly, along with practical suggestions for breathing into the possible steps to motivate me forward.

God Bless You, Angel Roger.

It brings me delight to know one of your deepest dreams came true. You met your life partner, have a new baby girl, Charlie, and are living a life as a happy family in Cambodia.

May everyday magic, miracles, and every expression of love and kindness accompany you for all the days of your life.

Love,

Junie

Dear Reader,

We all carry a child within us, tender, curious, and vulnerable, who sometimes feels unseen or unloved. This is my letter to my inner child, Noonie, the part of me who bore the weight of fear, shame, and neglect long before I could protect her. Writing to her, I am reminded of the power of compassion, presence, and play, and how reconnecting with that child can bring healing and joy. I share this intimate conversation to inspire you to embrace and nurture your own inner child.

Love,

Junie

Dearest Noonie,
  if you only knew...

My sweet inner child, Noonie, Junie... oh, precious child who lives inside of me. You sure didn't believe you were precious very often. You took on the projections that your mother, in her rage, carelessly threw at you, things no mother should ever say to her child, often accompanied with slaps or beatings and threats.

I'm so sorry, my loving little girl. I wish I could have been there for you right from the start. I wish the wise self, the higher mind, the loving adult that I have become could have cuddled you close when you were afraid, dried your tears, let you know how precious and important you are, and let you know that I will never leave you.

I'm here now, darling one. I'm here now, and I will never leave you. Know that what your mom said, as well as what your dad, your bother, Howard, and the others in the family said, had absolutely no bearing on who you are. They were misguided bullies. I'm so sorry they hurt you so badly.

How can I be there for you right now, sweet one? What would you like to say to me or ask me. What do you need from me, from the world?

Big Junie, there you are! I know you have come to me many times throughout our lifetime, and each time, it is the most wonderful thing. But you also go away a lot, and I feel alone and very lonely when you're not here. Please don't go away for so long anymore. I need to know you love me. I don't know why you go away, and then I feel small and like curling up and hiding.

Oh, sweetheart, I am so sorry for my absences. I want you to know that my absences are not a reflection of my lack of care or love for you. Still, no matter what, that's the effect they had on you, and that's not right; that's just not OK! I am so sorry!

So, dearest little Junie, I'm here, and I will talk to you every day. I will remind you that YOU are the best part of me. You want to know why? Because YOU, my darling, are my creativity. You are the writer, the poet, the singer, the artist, the one who loves music and dancing. You have a natural curiosity and tenderness for life. You love nature, animals, insects, and all of life.

No matter how harshly you were treated, you never lost your innocence or stopped caring for others who are hurting. Do you know how strong that makes you? And when you feel safe, you naturally shine your light and extraordinary talents into the world as though no one is watching. The operative words here are "when you feel safe." And the irony of that is, it seems I, also need to feel safe. So, I need you too, darling. Let's turn up the music and dance in every art form there is.

Let me ask you this, Noonie. Do you feel worthy and that you matter when you are writing?

YES!

Dancing?

YES!

Singing?

YES!

Coloring?

YES!

That's does it! Let's do at least one of those every day. OK? Let's remind each other that life can be fun, joyous, and easy. Let's finally take the time to play. We don't need to prove anything to anyone, my love. Let's start now. Wanna? What's your favourite song?

I don't know.

OK, one of them. Perhaps one we can dance to?

I Feel Good by James Brown!

Of course! You've got it.

I'm finding it and turning on my speaker. Let's dance, sweetheart. Is there something else you'd rather do or do as well?

I'd like to go outside with you. We haven't been outside yet today!

You got it!

And there's something else, sweetheart. Sometimes you may not feel like writing or singing or dancing or playing at all. Sometimes, being the highly sensitive child that you are, you just need to know that when things feel upsetting or bad, they will turn around. The sun will shine again.

And sometimes you will just need me to hold you close. I am tuned into you, my darling girl, and I will feel your sadness or fear or confusion and loneliness, and I promise you, my sweet inner child, I will hold you tight and reassure you that you are not alone. And together we will be held in the arms of God and know we are safe.

I love you so much, Noonalah, Noonie, Little Junie!

I love you, too, Big Junie.

OK... Let's find that song!

Love,

Big Junie, who loves you beyond measure—now and forever more.

Dear Reader,

Some people enter our lives and leave a mark that lasts forever. This letter is to my beloved Auntie Ethel, who was a guide, a champion, and a source of unwavering love throughout my life. She nurtured my earliest dreams, celebrated my successes, and offered comfort during my darkest days. Writing to her now, I reflect on her extraordinary heart and the ways she shaped the person I have become. I only wish I had made it on time and could have read her my letter and held her hand one last time.

Love,

Junie

Dearest Auntie Ethel,
  if only you knew...

It is fitting that I am beginning to collect my stories and letters in my latest book, *If You Only Knew: A Book of Healing Letters*, and that you are the one to whom I am writing now, just as I'm flying out to see you tomorrow, praying you are still alive so that I can hold your hand once more and read this letter to you and tell you one last time how much I love you.

You are the one, you know, who started me on my writing journey. I'll never forget the day you called me and told me look at the Toronto Telegram in the Family section. I ran to get the paper, and there was my poem! Imagine, my poem, right there in the "Have Your Say" column! I couldn't believe it! I was only eleven years old!

When I gave you the handwritten copy of my poem, I had no idea you were going to do that! But that's what you did and have always done. You champion others. You see the best in us, and you make sure we know it. You were always there, encouraging me to write, encouraging me to be the best of who I could be, and to believe in myself. Around you, it was easy to do. You showed me nothing but unconditional love each and every time we were together.

I remember when I was nineteen years old and living by myself in London, England. My best friend and I had parted ways a few months earlier, and I was in a terrible depression. You and Uncle Harold came to see me. As always, you held me in your tender embrace, told me that this too shall pass. I told you I wasn't ready to go home yet. You didn't try to dissuade me. Instead, you listened when I said that I wanted to go to Israel, work on a kibbutz, and have time to figure things out. You and Uncle Harold purchased my airline ticket and made sure I was safe in every way.

There are so many stories I could write about you, about us, and about Uncle Harold, your beloved husband who passed away so very young, leaving you alone with three beautiful children. I know he was your forever love, and you chose not to remarry. Instead, you put your heart and life into doing good deeds for others. It is your way.

It saddened me that while growing up and right to the end when Mom died, that she and you never saw eye-to-eye. Sisters. Such a shame. I learned early in my life that Mom was so very jealous of you. She always discouraged me from visiting you. She made me feel disloyal to her if I wanted to see you. I hated that. Like you, I'm an inclusive person, so it felt like a prison term, a life sentence to not be allowed to see you, my most favorite person in the world. I'm so sorry for that. But we always knew how much we loved each other.

You called me when Barbara, my beloved sister and best friend, died, and we cried together on the phone. You asked me in earnest if I thought my mother would accept a visit from you. You wanted to see her so much, to try to comfort her, to simply be together.

I answered honestly. "I don't know," I said. Do what feels right in your heart. And let us both pray that in her most anguished and vulnerable state, she will fall into your arms and whatever grievances have been will fall away."

"What is she so angry about? What have I done? I have lost count of how many times I have said I'm sorry, not even knowing what I am supposed to be sorry for."

I suggested that you ask yourself how it would make you feel going to visit her, knowing there was the risk of her not budging in her stance, or not going, and never knowing if she may have melted in your arms.

You said, "Noonalah, I'm on my way!" I was already at the house with Mom when you arrived, and it was as though every perceived wrongdoing disappeared upon her first glance of you. She gasped and sat up in her bed, where she had retreated in her pain. You ran to her side, and the two of you clung to one another as though your very lives depended on it. I left you both alone for hours and hours as you talked and wept and even dozed, wrapped around each other in her bed.

I wish I could say that your subsequent visits were as pure of heart, but Mom always had a way of misinterpreting things and finding fault. She simply didn't know how to maintain and sustain an open heart. I wish I knew what had happened in her young life that caused her to shut down, becoming so bitter and hard-hearted. I know you wish for that also, to know why she turned her back on you, her loving sister.

Then there were other times that she would open wide, so wide that you didn't think any more love and joy and beauty and wisdom and compassion were possible from one person. And then, without fail, she would flip to that other side again, the one with padlocks over her heart, and she would lash out instead. Anger seemed to be the safer way to go.

Both of us know the truth. The way she greeted you that day, like long-lost sisters, because, in fact, you were, is also who she really was, and you got to experience it, and so did I, and, well, so did she. Love is never lost, and that was pure, unconditional love, which can never be disputed. I hope you take that in and let it soothe and comfort you, my beautiful aunt.

You are the last of the Matriarchs of the Lazarus/Lebovici family from Romania. You've given the rest of us an ideal to live up to. How many people have you mentored in your life? Not just within our large family, most of them now gone, but hundreds over the decades of volunteering. You are always so positive in your outlook, always lending a helping hand.

You were the president of the B'nai Brith Women's Chapter. You delivered Meals on Wheels from the Baycrest Hospital and brought books from the library to the patients there. You always had a generous, loving smile to offer each person as you entered their room. Yes, I can imagine the kindness you delivered in every room you entered, which reminds me of one of my favorite recent memories of you from my visit last summer. Even at the age of 98, the bookmobile was still delivering books to your house each month—you had a pile to give back and you had read every one, cover to cover!

Oh my! I'm going to miss you so. I'm going to miss our many phone calls spanning three thousand miles across the continent over these past twenty years since I moved to the coast.

"Hello my Noonalah! How is my Noonalah?" You are the only one who still calls me that, just as you have from my earliest days. I don't think anything could replace the sound of one's nickname being spoken in the tenderest way from someone who loves you the way you loved me. You have been a bedrock for me, Auntie Ethel.

I was told that when they moved you into the nursing home last week, you fell, went unconscious, and are now in hospice. But before you lost consciousness, you were calling Uncle Harold's name and extended your arms to reach him. I know that he was right there when you reached out, and he is waiting with his wide-open arms and heart to welcome you back Home. As will Boobie and Pa, your beloved sister, Fran, and my mom. I believe my mom, from the heart of her spirit and soul, only knows love, and the two of you will embrace in a way that shall restore all that was lost. At least, that is my prayer.

I love you,

Noonalah

Dear Reader,

This letter is to my beloved Boobie, whose final days were filled with the quiet indignities of long-term care. Writing to her, I found myself weaving a story that bridges memory and imagination, honoring the vibrant woman she was while reimagining her passing in a way that feels tender and just. Through this letter, I hope to preserve her spirit, celebrate her life, and offer a vision of peace and joy beyond the confines of suffering. It is both an act of grief and an act of love.

Love,

Junie

Dearest Boobie,
  if only you knew...

I wish there had been another way for you to die. Languishing in long-term care, among all those old people whose lives had been reduced to endless days locked in their dying bodies, unable to move on. You didn't deserve that. No one does. It is the worst Purgatory.

I have written you a story, a new story of your death, as a way to grieve the loss of you from my life. My greatest wish for you, for all of us, is if it could have been like this:

Sylvia put down the phone with a sigh. Margie and Fred would be here in half an hour. She looked around the kitchen once more. Where did she put her purse? How many years had she lived here, exactly? She couldn't remember—over forty for sure. Raised all of her kids in this house. Watched her husband die here, too. *I'll soon join him*, she thought to herself. *The time has come. I won't live long in that place they are taking her to. No bloody way!* But she's been compliant, cheerful even. Why not? What choice did they give her? That's what they do with old people, isn't it? They did it to her grandmother. Her own parents escaped it by dying before ever suffering the indignity.

She slowly shuffled to the bathroom. *Damn*, she thought, *if only I could walk faster, run, fly, yes, fly the way I do in so many of my dreams. Those dreams seem to last longer these days. I wonder if this is what happens when you're this old, just a matter of leaving your body somewhere and finally tearing loose.* How she wished with all her might she could do that now, before her kids showed up.

"Here it is." She said out loud to herself. Talking to herself again! She knew it was there. Picking up her purse, she announced to the empty bathroom, "See, there's nothing wrong with my mind!"

She reached into her purse and found the black and gold tube of cherry red lipstick and reflected on how she had worn that same Revlon brand since she was a girl, and always cherry red. Applying it now with deliberate motion to her thin lips, she smiled, thinking of all the times she watched her mother applying her lipstick perfectly without a mirror.

"How do you do that?" she always asked. "Simple, I know where my lips are!" her mother would reply, and they would burst out laughing.

My, how she missed her mother's spirit, her laughter, the smell of her cooking. The fun they'd have together. There will be no fun now.

A chill moved through her. *Why can't they leave me alone? I'll refuse to go, that's all. Now don't go and upset yourself. Oh, look at you!* She gazed critically at her reflection in the mirror and combed back her wisps of white hair. Her hand was almost steady. She knew that inside this confused old woman's face was someone much younger, intelligent, and alive. If only her body would respond to her mind's commands. She'd be out of here so fast.

Moving slowly back into the kitchen, trying to ignore the pictures, ornaments, and treasures she would probably never see again, she lowered herself into her favorite armchair by the window to sit and wait. She smoothed down her pleated skirt and gazed out.

The wind was blowing the autumn leaves to and fro. Another chill ran through her frail body. She thought back to her grandmother. She thought of her constantly these days, vivid flashbacks to that affluent street in Forest Hill that embraced stately hundred-year-old oaks, maples, and aristocratic houses. Walking down that glorious street, one would never suspect such a hell house was among them. But it was, and she dreaded going there.

It was where the old, sick, and dying people were put, the wealthy ones, that is. Give them a sense that they weren't going out too far from where they came in. She hated it there. Who were these people? Once healthy, prosperous, respected, with homes, families, and comings and goings. Who were they now? And the stench of urine, halitosis, and unwashed bodies mingled with antiseptic cleaners assaulted her nostrils the moment she stepped inside.

Wheelchairs, and chairs covered in corduroy with overstuffed, lumpy pillows, carrying the frames of fragmented men and women, lined up against the walls of the foyer. Some were positioned in front of the picture window and so they could gaze out at the people passing by who were oblivious to their searching or vacant stares.

As she passed the lineup of crumpled bodies, Sylvia would try to become invisible, avoiding eye contact as she hurried to the elevator. But sometimes, an awful, sickly cough or a haunting laugh would shatter her imposed focus, and the armour she was wearing would crumble. Sometimes a kindly voice would say, "Nice dress, honey. Where'd you buy it?" She could never look into the woman's pathetic eyes.

On some level, the pain this poor woman must have to be conscious in this God forsaken place, knowing there was no escape, was Sylvia's pain too, and she couldn't bear it. "Have a nice day," was the most she could mutter, and even that came out as a coughed-up whisper as she waited for the elevator, holding her breath.

Waiting for that miserably slow elevator was like a death sentence imposed on the young and vibrant. No clocks ticked in the foyer to mark the time it took for the elevator to reach the first floor. Empty time, vacuous faces. No one cared that even when it finally did arrive, it would stop at every damn floor all the way to the top, even when no one else was getting on or off.

Finally, Boobie's floor. The worst. More pungent smells. This ward was not only for the sick and dying but also for the insane. Here, there was no escaping the screaming wails that could turn into hysterical laughter from rooms she never wanted to enter.

And the lineup along the walls of men and women was prominent in this corridor as well. Only here were they strapped into their chairs. Some tried to get out and were grotesquely hanging over one side as they squirmed and moaned with inhuman sounds. What the hell is my grandmother doing in here? Sylvia thought each time she came to visit.

Sylvia blinked back to the present and shuddered. The wind seemed to have picked up while she had been remembering. The leaves continued to blow. She wrapped her ivory shawl around her thin shoulders. She noticed some school children kicking about the leaves across the street, laughing. But her mind was already back in the old folks' home.

God... is there a God? Then get my Boobie out of here. So what if she is sick? Even incontinent like the others. But that's where it stopped. Her Boobie had a mind. She can't be here. She'll die here. Doesn't anyone care? Please. Somebody, anybody.

Wiping away the tears already streaming down her young face and trying to summon a smile, she entered her grandmother's room. And there was Boobie, so frail and tiny in the oversized bed. She looked so much older and shriveled from the week before. She wasn't speaking now. She lay motionless.

"Boobie, it's me, Sylvia," praying she'd look up and look at her with intelligent eyes, and together they'd make a plan of escape. But she didn't. Bobbie had only been there for two weeks, but now she was waiting to die and didn't want to be rescued.

A sudden noise jolted Sylvia back to the present. She stretched her face to the glass and peered out the window. What was it? Then she saw her son and daughter pull up in front of the house.

"Oh my god, it's time," she whispered in a voice she didn't recognize. Suddenly, a pain seized her chest, and she fell forward.

As Sylvia looked around her, she realized that she was in that horrible place, in Bobbie's room, but this time there was an exquisite light, and Bobbie was suddenly there, sitting up in her bed and reaching towards her, laughing her beautiful laugh. Those intelligent eyes were not just smiling; they were sparkling with such humour. Sylvia could hardly contain herself. A sense of peace and joy so magnificent and unlike anything she had ever known enveloped her. Her Boobie's room dissolved around them, and Sylvia felt herself being lifted high above her beloved home. She was with her Boobie, and they were dancing among the clouds. And was that mom in the distance, in the light...?

Margie and Fred stepped out of the car and noticed their mother sitting in her favorite chair by the window.

"Looks like she's fallen asleep," Fred said gently to his sister. "Yeah, she looks so peaceful," Margie replied. "It's too bad we have to wake her to face what will probably be the worst day of her life. I hate what we're doing, Fred. I just hate it."

"Me too, Marge. But we've been over this a million times. There's no choice. Neither of us lives in the city. She refuses to move, and she simply can't look after herself anymore. What choice do we have?"

Fred helped his sister up the stairs, opened the door to their childhood home, and walked in.

Oh, my Boobie, how I wish this were what your last day had been like. But Syvia is me, and those are my memories of how you lived your final weeks on this earth. Can we change the past by simply rewriting it? I hope so, for this is what I would wish for you, and for me when my time comes; to dance above the world among the clouds as you bring me Home.

I love you Boobie,

Love,

Junie

Dear Reader,

This letter is to my father, written at a time when he needed to feel the love and care that had always been at the heart of our relationship. I wanted him to know, in every word, how much he had shaped my life, supported me, and loved me unconditionally, even when I may not have fully understood him. Writing to him became a way to wrap him in my gratitude, admiration, and prayers, offering comfort when words spoken aloud might not have been enough. It is a love letter, a tribute, and a reminder that the bond between a father and daughter can hold strength, tenderness, and healing across all the years.

Love,

Junie

Dearest Dad,
  if you only knew...

Before you read on, I'm going to ask two things of you. First, please allow yourself to open up to me by feeling the love I have for you, because I am writing to you now with all my love. Second, please keep these pages between us. Of course, if you want to share this with Mom, you certainly can, but please, no one else. Mom understands me well, and this is my attempt to help you know me even better.

As you must know, you are constantly in my thoughts and in my prayers these days. There are so many things I want to say to you, but sometimes it doesn't come out the way I want, so I thought I would try to write you a letter that you can read at your leisure, in quiet privacy, and keep with you always.

Dad, I want you to know, not just how much I love you and respect you because I believe you know this, but to tell you how lucky and blessed I have always felt because you are my father. You are an exemplary model of a father, for you have always, always been there for me.

I'll never forget those horrible, terrifying times that I was sick with debilitating depression, and it was your love and mom's that pulled me through. I'll never forget how, in your quiet, gentle way, you would reach over and hold my hand and squeeze it tightly. You would often tell me I was too sensitive for my own good and must learn not to let people hurt me so much.

Your support during those times meant more to me than words could ever express. Or the times I've been confused and not known what to do with my life, and how you would encourage me, not always with words of advice, but by instilling confidence in me that I could do anything, and to trust that things would work out well.

Financial assistance was always given without question, even when you were having difficulties. You always came through, Dad. You've always shown me how important I am to you. That trip to Puerto Vallarta three years ago with me and Mom was the most loving gift you could ever give me. You forfeited your own very much needed vacation by sending me instead, and I'll never, ever forget that. I came home from that trip better than I had in a very long time.

There have been so many things, little and big, that you have done for me, and I'm so grateful to you for all of it. There have been lots of times, perhaps too many, when I haven't understood you or misinterpreted you or haven't given you a chance to express yourself the way you know how. I've often gotten angry, impatient, and obstinate with you, but I always knew you were thinking of my best interests. Of course, your thoughts on what is best for me and mine don't always jive, but I wish I could have shown you more patience and more acceptance for what you had to say.

I guess it's all a learning process, and people don't always have to agree to love each other. And that's what I want you to know, how much I do love you and respect you.

Dad, I've never known another person who worked as hard as you have. Always carrying on two or three jobs at a time to make sure your wife and family were all looked after. So many times, I watched you come home late at night or the early hours of the morning looking so tired and so weary, and yet you were up the next morning before anyone else, coffee percolating, dressed and ready for a full day ahead. And I never heard you complain. I never did.

I've also never known a more loving man to his wife. Throughout all of your arguments and misunderstandings, I don't think I've ever seen a stronger union, a stronger friendship. I often wish I would find a man to love me like you love Mom—so willing to be there in so many ways.

It's a different world today, Dad, and many women, including me, find their own way in life. Our identities often come through the career we have chosen, as well as the efforts we put into our friends and homes.

For me, this is extremely satisfying. I want you to know this. I love my life so far. Although I know how happy it would make you to see me married and with a family, I want to assure you that, whether that will be my life or not, I am quite content as I am. Being married is not a goal for me. I guess if it were, I would have already been, because, as we know, I have had several opportunities.

My life seems to have taken a different path because of my nature and what I need to fulfill. Years ago, when friends were getting married and having babies, my joy and excitement came from traveling and learning about different countries and people. And always, always, learning more about myself.

The career path I'm embarking upon now is truly the most exciting focus I have ever had. It seems so natural for me to be pursuing a career in psychotherapy. I know I am good with people. I have endured many painful internal struggles and learned from them. And I am still successfully learning to overcome them with ease, stability, and maturity. I yearn to share this knowledge, and the beauty that life holds, and to cherish the gift of being alive, which is the best thing I have to offer.

It's been through witnessing the struggles you and mom have endured that I have learned this precious gift of hanging in and hanging on. Through every hardship, you and Mom have found your way through and restored peace to your lives. The determination, the love, and the attitude of "one day at a time" and things will get better have given me the strength I've needed so many, many times.

And that brings me pretty well to what I've been wanting to say to you the most, and that is, please, Dad, don't give up the fight. I know you're going through the hardest time you've ever encountered, and I don't think you have ever felt worse, but Dad, please hang in there. I believe in miracles. I believe everything is possible, and maybe if you think it too, and then the love we all have for you could bring about the best scenario possible, and you'll pull through this. That would be the greatest of miracles!

And, Dad, even more than this, I pray you will be more patient with yourself. Tonight, you were so upset, and it took so much out of you. Howard meant well when he was adjusting your oxygen. Sometimes it's so damn hard watching someone you suffer so much. We want to do anything, anything at all to make you feel a little more comfortable. Try and let us. You've given to each of us all of your life. Why not relax and let us take care of you for a while in whatever small way we can? That's what life's all about. That's what families are all about.

You are so loved by all of us. If only you could relax in the comfort of that knowledge. Some excellent advice you've given me throughout my life is, "Don't let so many things bother you." Dad, heed your own words. The only thing to think about now is getting well again and coming home.

I love you so much,

Junie
XXXXXXX

Dear Reader,

This letter is to Alan, the boy who touched my heart in ways I have carried with me for decades. I am writing not just to remember him, but to speak across the years—to reach out to a young love lost far too soon, and to process the grief, guilt, and longing that have shaped my life ever since. These words are meant to honor him, to ask for forgiveness, and to seek understanding for the patterns his death left behind. I hope, through this letter, that he can hear me, as if time itself could bend, and that in reading it, others may glimpse the ways early love, loss, and trauma imprint on my life. It is a conversation across time, a dialogue of heart, memory, and enduring affection.

Love,

Junie

Dearest Alan,
  if you only knew...

We were kids, really, young teens when we met. You were the rich, cute Bad Boy, the one who lived in Forest Hill, went to some school for juvenile delinquents, and would show up at the Neptune/Wasdale park where all of us, not-so-rich kids, hung out. Several of us girls had crushes on you. Sonja wore your ring for a while. You were sweet. I always wondered what you did that would have sent you to a school for wayward kids. I don't remember interacting with you too much, not until we met up in Florida when we were seventeen.

It was Easter break, and I was there with my parents when you wandered into the restaurant where we were having dinner. I was mortified to see you. It wasn't you; it was me. I hated my life and wanted to disappear from the earth. I hated you seeing me in that state and, more than anything, seeing how I looked. I believed at the time that I was fat, ugly, and unlovable.

I had met Freddie about two weeks before going to Florida. He was the first boy in my young life who seemed to care for me. Like really and genuinely care. It didn't seem to matter to him that I was fat and failing in school. He didn't seem to care that I was chronically depressed. He wanted to make me laugh. He wanted to make me happy, and he succeeded at doing both. We spent every minute we could together, right up to the day I reluctantly got on a plane headed for Miami Beach.

My parents thought it would be good for me to have a 'holiday'. What were they thinking? They sent me to Esther's Brasiers on Bathurst Street to get a couple of custom-made bathing suit tops, because even the biggest department stores, like Eaton's and Simpsons, didn't have my cup size. I was a friggin' freak! But

Freddie didn't seem to care about that. We promised to write every day. I told him I'd write first to give him the address of the hotel where we were staying as I didn't know it before we left.

The day you came sauntering into the restaurant, Alan, I had already been in Florida almost two weeks. I had written to Freddy every day and had not heard back even once. Not once. I was disheartened and had fallen back into how I felt before I met him, believing happiness was something other people had. That fun was something other teens experienced. That lasting love was not for girls who looked like me.

Much to my chagrin, Mom and Dad invited you to join us at our table. You were as witty and charming as ever. You had the gift of the gab. I sat quietly, not out of politeness but because I had nothing to say. You asked me if I wanted to go for a walk. I wanted to hide in my bed. But my parents thought you were sweet, and there were three against one in favour of the walk.

So, we walked and you talked. You told me that you always had a special feeling for me. I thought, *Here goes, I wonder what beach we're going to end up at with my pants down and his penis shoved into me.* Pretty gross, but hey, that's what I knew I was good for. I had twelve years of proof. Boys, men wanted one thing only, and I gave it to them. I was only five years old when I was first indoctrinated into the land of child sin. After that, it just became normal.

Anyway, we walked, and you kept talking, telling me you thought I had the most loving heart of anyone you had ever known. And that I was so pretty. Now I really wanted to throw up. Pretty? Did you have special magnifying glasses that allowed you to see under the mountains of fat? Was there really a slim girl trapped inside? Anyway, I didn't believe a word you were saying, Alan. And yet, you seemed so sincere. So gentle. And you weren't leading me onto some darkened beach or the back alley of some building somewhere. But where were you leading me?

When I told you that I wasn't planning on going back to Toronto with my parents but had entertained thoughts of running away, you led me to this seedy part of Miami where hookers and strippers hung out.

"What are we doing here, Alan?"

You told me that if I didn't go home with my parents and was really planning on running away, this is where I would end up. I hated you more than anything in that moment. You were still being gentle.

"Junie," you said, "look at you. You will be walking down the street and some slimeball from one of these burlesque houses will spot you, offer you a job, good money, you will need the money, you already hate yourself, so you wouldn't give a shit, take the job, and well..."

"Take that back!" I shrieked, "I would never do that! Take me back to my hotel right now, Alan!"

And so, you did. You turned around, walked me back, but kept on talking. You went on to say that you wanted to go steady with me, that when we both returned to Toronto, you wanted to look after me. That you didn't know what had happened to me, but whatever it was, you were going to help turn it around. You understood that life can be really hard sometimes, but it doesn't have to be that way forever. "Tell me you will go steady with me, Junie."

I finally spoke. "Are you crazy, Alan? No. I am not telling you that." I didn't know what your game was. You still weren't trying to get into my pants. You just kept telling me that you wanted to be my boyfriend and that you would take care of me.

I didn't have the nerve, Alan, to tell you that I met someone a few weeks earlier who I thought really cared, and that I couldn't go steady with you because I was praying this guy meant it. I needed to return to Toronto and see for myself. I couldn't tell you that. But more, I couldn't figure you out.

When you wouldn't let me go into my hotel room—not forcefully but insistently—until I agreed to go steady, I blurted out, "Fine!" Before I could run into the hotel, you lifted me in the air, saying, "I'll be good to you, I promise, I will. And I'll come by tomorrow morning before I head back to Toronto with my friends."

No one could have predicted what happened next. No one. When I finally came up to my room, I found a note on my bed. It was from my mom saying that Freddie had called me twice while

I was on my walk with Alan. He had just received all my letters. Apparently, I had sent them to the wrong address. I was in shock and equally elated! I got down on my knees and cried. "Thank you, God. It was real. It is real. He really does care."

Back in Toronto, Freddie and I resumed our relationship, and I had never felt happier. But you kept pursuing me. I didn't answer your phone calls. Finally, finally, I met with you and told you the truth. You looked so disheartened. I felt like shit. A week or so later, you told me you were going to go with your friend on his business trip to Vancouver. He was driving, and it would be an opportunity to give you some space and time to try and get over me. You asked if you could come to say goodbye. I said, of course! It never happened. You came while I was in my bedroom, probably on the phone with Suki. It was late, and Norman, my sister Barbara's boyfriend, answered the door and sent you away, telling him I didn't accept callers at 10 pm.

I never hated anyone more than I did Norman in that moment. And I had every reason to hate him as he was one of my abusers. The next morning, your friend, Andy, with whom you were driving to Vancouver, called me to say what a consistent bitch I was. That you had come to say goodbye, and I wouldn't let you in.

"I don't know what your game is, June, but all he wants to do is be kind to you. To love you. Anyway, he's determined to see you before we leave and wants to know if you are willing to let us pick you up and drive you to school so he can at least see you for a few minutes.

"Yes, yes, of course,"

"Okay, we'll be there in a little while."

When Andy arrived, you weren't with him. He told me you thought I'd be late for school since he had a few errands to do before coming to get me, and the timing just wouldn't work. So, Andy drove me to school instead.

"Listen, he sends his love and says good-bye. The guy's got it bad for you. I wish you had let him see you last night. Seems like you just keep letting him down."

I got out of the car with Andy still lecturing me.

I never did say goodbye to you, and I didn't trust Andy to tell you the truth about what happened, so I felt lousy about the whole thing. I hoped that in a few weeks, when you came home, I could tell you what had happened at my door that night and that you'd forgive me. Even if I couldn't be your girlfriend, I wanted to be your friend if you'd let me. But I had no way to reach you, to explain. There were no cell phones in those days. No, I had to wait until you returned from Vancouver.

You never got to Vancouver. You never returned. Ever.

The next morning, I slept late. I was awakened by the phone. It was Sonia.

"June, are you sitting down?"

"I'm lying down. I'm still asleep."

"Wake up, sweetie, I've got some awful news."

"What is it, Sonia?" By this time, I was starting to sit up.

"I just spoke to Alan's friend, Andy. They had a car accident. June, Alan was killed."

"WHAT?! NO!" I screamed. "NO, NO, PLEASE, NO!"

"June, I'll be right there. I'm sorry. I'm so sorry. I'm coming over."

I couldn't stop screaming. Mom and Dad came tearing into my room. I told them what happened. They tried to console me but couldn't. I wouldn't be consoled. It was my fault. If I had only told you the truth earlier. If I had only been nicer to you, maybe you wouldn't have had to go off to Vancouver. You said to me that's why you were going, to get over me. Now you were dead. DEAD! No, it couldn't be. I had never experienced anyone's death before.

My Auntie Channa died when I was about eight, but I hardly knew her, nor really understood it. But I understood the finality of death when my precious budgie, Elvis, died when I was twelve. But you were the first person to die to whom I had ever been that close. It wasn't fair. It couldn't be true. You couldn't be dead. It was April 30th and your 18th birthday.

Within a very short time, the apartment filled up with my friends. Freddie stayed right by my side. Suki, Sonia, Pam, Carrel, Melonie, others. That same evening, there was a knock at the door. It was Andy. He just got back and wanted to tell me personally what happened. He said you were on the highway approaching Sault Ste. Marie, when you saw the sign for Wa-Wa.

He said you were driving. He went on to say:

"Alan said, 'That sign reminds me of June. She always goes, Wah-Wah-Wah when she doesn't hear you.' At that exact moment, he lost control of the car and hit a pole at top speed. I thought you might want to know he was thinking of you right to the end."

If I hadn't felt guilty before this, these words sealed it for me. It wasn't until several years later that I learned the absolute truth, which was that you weren't driving at all. It was Andy who was behind the wheel. He somehow lost control, and you were thrown from the car. It was very cruel of Andy to make up that lie, but I guess it was the only thing he knew to do to assuage his guilt about what really happened. He was already angry with me, and perhaps this was his way of getting back. He did an excellent job. I became completely despondent.

Now, at seventy-five, I am beginning to consciously realize the hopes and dreams I buried inside of myself when you died. I am still seeking clarity and truth. I came to believe that nothing good would ever happen to me, and if it did, it would never last. I believed I was responsible for your death, and to love someone would mean something terrible happening to them. To both of us. To accept someone else's love would lead to a tragic death.

My brother-in-law, Allan, told me over and over again every time he abused me, "If you tell Lorraine, it will kill her." My sister, Lorraine, was nine and a half years older than me. She adored me. It was like I was her baby from the time we were born. And she was my best friend. And her husband was having sex with me. I was only ten and in my little girl understanding, I felt sorry for him to be in such a dilemma. "I'm in love with two girls. I don't know what to do," he said each time he was molesting me.

If I didn't hate myself already, oh boy, I despised myself now. He was right. It would kill her. I would never tell. I stopped looking her in the eyes. I stopped going over to babysit because it meant he would drive me home and tell her he'd be going to his photography studio on the way. He failed to tell her he'd take me there first.

I have never had a long-term loving relationship. I married David only 2 ½ years ago, and he left me while I was battling cancer. It's way too complicated to know all the reasons why every romance that I thought would be forever turned out in major heartbreak. What I know for sure now is that I took on some false beliefs about romance, which I applied to myself when I was just a little girl.

By the time I was in my mid-twenties, I had it pretty dug in that I did not deserve more than to be abused. But I was still looking for love, as they say, in all the wrong places. But surely, it was your death, and the only reason you died other than it was your destiny to do so, was because I sent you away. When I finally told you I was seeing Freddie and what had happened with my letters to him, you went away to 'get over me.' And you were killed on the way, apparently with my name on your lips, when you lost control of the car. At least that was what Andy told me. It makes sense that I took on the belief that nothing good ever lasts, and worse than that, anyone who attempts to love me will end up with misery, pain, or even death.

Nothing will bring you back, Alan. But I'm reaching out to you now. Imagine that, over half a century later, I am still struggling with wanting, needing to know true love–lasting love. Am I delusional? Love can come at any age. I want and need to know it is possible to know someone cherishes me and makes me their number one. And beyond that, right now, on these pages, I am asking for your forgiveness. It's time, while I'm still alive, to let go of the pattern that started from the belief I took on the night you tragically died.

Back then, even Freddie's loving nature, his kindness, and adoration didn't take me out of the clinical depression I went into after you died. It's taken until now, in this letter to you, to ask you wholeheartedly for forgiveness. Can you forgive me, Alan? Please, come through me now on these pages and speak to me.

I love you, my forever friend,

Junie

Oh, Junie, Enough! Yes, hear me, feel me, allow me in now. Thank you for reaching out to me. There is NOTHING to forgive, dear one. You were innocent. I was innocent. It was my destiny to leave the earth at such a young age, and it's how Life plays out sometimes. My death became a catalyst for the learning and evolution of many people. You need to know that I did love you. Your concern about not being pretty or slim enough was not anywhere in my mind. I saw your heart. I mean, I really saw it. There was nothing superficial about you.

We were only teenagers, but you stood out among all the rest. I was always attracted to your goodness and your innocence, and I have been a guardian angel among countless others for you ever since that fated night. I have watched you put your heart and soul into everything you do, whether it's in your career and the thousands of people you have helped, or your friendships or family members. You give it all. You can stop explaining, defending, and trying to prove to anyone who you are. You are about to see a very different life going forward.

In a year from now, you won't recognize where you are. You are so loved, valued, and cherished. You are a magnificent being, and a magnificent future awaits you. You are at the toughest place right now. Hang in, dearest One.

Also, you need to know that you had every reason not to want to tell me about Freddie when we met that fateful night when we were both only 17. You hadn't heard from him, but you still had hope that you would, which is why you couldn't say anything. Under all of it, from that time until the day I died, you were innocent. You simply didn't have the skills to communicate that you had a boyfriend. You thought by not telling me, you were protecting me. I know you've grown lightyears since then. Today you teach communication skills. What did we know back then? Who were your role models? And I was always chasing girls and getting what I wanted from them but was left empty in the end. I was a Bad Boy, which is why I was sent to a school for juvenile delinquents. I protested everything I didn't think was fair, hoping someone would listen. Your heart and my heart were twin souls, and they still are.

We are also multidimensional beings, so there will be a time soon that we will meet beyond the veil and you will feel and experience the bliss of unconditional love always present in that dimension. You will bring it back to where you are now, and well, honey, you can tap into it now and always. You can live in this dimension as often as you like. Your brilliant stories will be reborn again. Celebrate, dearest Junie. You've earned it.

I am aware of your body pain, your loneliness, of feeling stuck, and not knowing where to go or what to do. Hang in there, beautiful Junie, you are NOT alone. I know you can't see me, but feel me, OK? Feel the sincerity of my words. This is not a pep talk. It's a sincere message from my infinite heart to yours. Know you are being cared for even during these latest challenges. Know you are being loved and you are protected. The Universe, God, Your Angels, too many to count, the Archangels are guiding you, guarding you, holding and embracing you. Breathe this in. Call on me day and night. Call any of us.

I love you, Junie. I always will, and I know you love me too. Our love is eternal.

Yours always,

Alan

Dear Reader,

This letter is to Deborah, a soul who taught me the depths of courage, creativity, and love in a way that has stayed with me across the years. I am writing to honor her, to witness her life, and to speak to her now, even though she has left this world, asking for forgiveness, gratitude, and closure. These words are a testament to the bond we shared, a bridge between teacher and student, friend and sister, heart to heart. I hope, through this letter, Deborah can feel the love, sorrow, and admiration I carry, as if time itself could bend so our spirits could meet. It is a conversation across the eternal, a dialogue of memory, love, and reverence.

Love,

Junie

Dearest Deborah,
    if only you knew...

I am listening to Ave Maria over the phone that another dear soul, my writing buddy, Deborah Seidman, is playing for me from her home in Taos, New Mexico. Earlier, when I heard her introduction to this song, talking about the divine feminine, passion, peace, and purity, it brought me to these pages. I leaped from my chair and onto my computer, where I am writing to you, finally, with my heart wide open. Ave Maria is still reverberating throughout my whole being and bringing me to you, where you remain alive. And you greet me here. You are also greeting me with an open heart and, beyond that, a tender smile, full acceptance, forgiveness, and light. Thank you! Oh, yes, thank you! I have been so burdened for letting you down.

I know that you understand, and so perhaps this letter is to myself in some way. A time for self-forgiveness. I only want to remember us the way we were, once we melted away the boundaries of teacher and student and became sisters, dancing this way and that, in this crazy, wonderful, mixed-up, and mysterious world together.

I will never forget the first time I laid eyes on you. I would never have known you were an acclaimed composer and vocal coach. How could I have known when you walked into my home on the first day of a new writing circle and introduced yourself to me in an almost apologetic way? You were not quite sure you should be here. You were not quite sure if you could write, but thought you would like to give it a try.

I felt your humility along with a captivating presence. The kind that enfolds a person when they look into the eyes of a wise woman, a shaman, a teacher of the highest order. You carried a presence and a dignity that was both regal and simple at the same time. An impossible mix, yet we were able to hold each with equanimity, without any pretense. Even later, when you were very sick, even when you were the most vulnerable a person can be, you remained noble and gracious.

On that first night when you wrote from an exercise I offered and then tentatively shared what you had written, the silence that followed was breathtaking. It was the kind of silence you experience in a concert hall after a performance of the highest caliber. That all-consuming inhalation when the audience becomes one entity that can no longer hold its breath, and so it explodes into a torrent of thunderous applause. It was like that after you read, and I wanted to leap to my feet and give you a standing ovation. I think we all did.

And I probably would have if I were sitting in the circle beside you and was not the teacher. Your writing continued to evoke that same response week after week until you began to trust your voice on the page despite a lifetime of doubt. Children's stories, poetry, prose, song lyrics, and memoirs came tumbling out of you in the same way a parched and starving person would grab and clutch a flask of water and then gulp it down. Each piece seemed to be written as though it would be your last.

You were writing as though your life depended on it, and it did. You were writing for your life. For a long time, it was only me who knew the demon you were fighting. I wondered if you were going to share it with the others in our circle. It seemed awkward that you didn't with the intimacy that was present. I never questioned your choice. I just wondered. And then one night, you arrived late, looking disheveled and very pale with make-up that tried to cover a face tormented by pain. I rose to greet you and hug you, and wished that hug could melt away the hopelessness I read in your eyes.

You sat down and tried to smile, but the mask cracked, and you wept, and you told the group that you had stage four cancer and that you had just come from seeing the doctor who told you to get your affairs in order.

You courageously tried to summon the brave part of you and declared that you were going to fight just like you had for the last four years. You told us that you were not supposed to have lived beyond six months when you got the first prognosis. But then, in an almost inaudible whisper, you said you were not as confident this time.

You continued to come to our groups, sometimes having to miss them because of the fatigue and nausea from the treatments. But you continued to write. And then write more. Writing became your devoted spiritual practice. You were reaching in to find the voice that you privately tucked away to survive all those years ago. Buried deep within you were secrets and pain no one would ever know about once you took your place on the stage as an internationally acclaimed composer, conductor, performer, and voice coach.

And on top of that, you donned a quick wit and wild sense of humor that could bring the house down equally as when you were performing. After sixteen years of an illustrious career in Europe, you returned home to Victoria to make your name here. Of course, I tell myself you moved back so we could meet. How else could I have met you? And had I not, it would have been a terrible loss in my life—not to know one who loves as deeply as you.

At first sight, I felt a sense of familiarity. I knew immediately our relationship would be more than teacher and student. And later, when the group was over and you asked to continue privately, of course, I said yes. And so, you did and began writing with a vengeance, telling stories of your life you never dared to tell before, memories purging out of you about people and events never revealed to another living soul. You were ready and felt safe enough to unburden, sister to sister, friend to friend, soul to soul. You were willing to tell it all until the suffering of the past would become stories of strength and heroism.

When your body became increasingly frail, writing became your prayer, your way to God. And our visits became less about your book and more about two people needing one another. For me, it was to give all that I could to a friend whom I loved. For you, it was having me hold you as you sobbed, when the terror took over, when you knew you had to surrender to this vicious beast that was devouring your body, when more than anything else in the world, you wanted to live. You had to, you said. You needed to leave your legacy, your book, what you now understood. If it were to help even one other person, you said that is all that mattered.

The book took a dramatic shift from teaching people how to sing, a user-friendly, "how to book" about what you had learned about the body and posture, vocal cords, and breathing techniques, and became a book of the heart, daring to tell parts of your own story. How, as a child, your voice was stripped away bit by bit. It was a book about who you were and who you have become.

Your hand couldn't move fast enough across the page to share how vital it was to speak your truth, reclaim your voice, your power, and ultimately your life. It felt like a desperate act. The longing was so great. And that's how it ended. The curtain came down before the last chapter got written. Before the dream was ever realized.

I miss you, my friend. And I need to tell you, finally, I am sorry. I am so sorry for not being able to tell you back then why I couldn't continue to see you and why our private lessons had to end when you still needed me so much. The truth was, dear Deborah, I, too, was dying. A different kind of death, but a death all the same. The death of my spirit, my joie de vivre, of all I knew of life, of friends and laughter, ocean walks, love, and meaningful work. Instead, the curse returned, the unrelenting suicidal ideation, anxiety, and crippling depression of what I have come to call the torture chamber of my mind, part of my diagnosis of bipolar affective disorder.

This is when hope feels like the farthest thing from my truth. Yet, how on earth could I tell you that! You, who were really dying, your body disappearing in front of me. How could I tell you then that I, too, was dying in my own way? My dying was filled with shame, the kind that comes from the stigmas around this insidious, crippling disease. I learned at a young age to put on a tight mask so no one would know I was suffering inside.

But now the mask was crumbling, and I couldn't let you see it. I don't know what lame excuse I used. I only remember how you gasped, and swallowed tears, trying desperately to understand. The only other thing I remember is it split my heart open to tell you I could no longer be there for you. I sank into an even larger pit of self-loathing, but I swear, Deborah, I didn't have another ounce of energy to give anyone. I was barely getting myself out of bed then.

It couldn't have been worse timing. And from that day, until now, even though we would see each other again, the guilt I have carried has been enormous. I know it is time to forgive myself; it is long overdue. I know you have forgiven me. I just wish we had met as children and were best friends so we could have shared a lifetime instead of the time we had.

Deborah, you made a magnificent impact on this earth. I hope you know that. You were so brave, and beautiful, and talented, and funny! And you were a gift to me. And I obviously was to you, too.

Here I am typing on the very same computer where you put your fingers when we had our closure on the last day of our sacred writing circle. We were reading out the letters we had written, which expressed our appreciation for one another. You waited to be last. Then you went to my computer and put on a Leonard Cohen song "Dance Me to the End of Love." When it was over, you said, "Junie, this is my gift for you. This is what you do for us. You write us to the end of love."

Now I remember our last time together. Our walk in Beacon Hill Park. It was a beautiful, glorious day. You told me you weren't afraid anymore. You said to me that you had come to peace with your life and that you had been seeing a minister at your church, and he was helping. I could feel that to be true. You truly had a peacefulness about you. We planned to meet again in a few weeks after I returned from California. You invited me to your home, wanted me to see Gaston again, your beautiful, fat, regal cat whom you adored.

I called you as soon as I got back to confirm our meeting. Someone else answered your phone. She told me you died two days ago. I hung up the phone, and I wept. It has taken me this long to write. Has it been a year? More? I do know you were looking forward to leading the Getting Higher Choir at their performance at the Alex Goolden Hall. And I was told you did it. There is a video of that evening. I watched it, and it was shocking to see you being held up, supported to get up the few steps onto the stage. You were so ill. But one tenet you upheld to the very end is that the show must go on.

And on it went.

You died the next day.

What a hero. I wonder if you were at your Celebration of Life. I hope so. And maybe it was good you were where you were, because there were no more seats left in the hall! I hope you heard the choir as they lifted their voices to the heavens for you. I was there and listened to dozens of people who came up and shared their personal adventures of you. Paid their tributes to you. Do you have any idea how many lives you touched? What an enormous life you led? How brave you were? And how grateful I am to have known you, to have loved you?

Without a doubt in my heart, I know we will see each other again and will continue where we left off, holding each other to the end of eternity, to the end of love.

God bless you, Deborah.
With all of my heart,

Junie

Dear Reader,

This final letter is to my mother; a woman whose life and love shaped me in ways I am only now fully beginning to understand. Ours was a complicated relationship. I write to honor her, to witness her courage, and to hold her memory close, even though she has left this world. These words are an offering of forgiveness, gratitude, and remembrance, a way to reconcile the complexity of love, loss, and longing that marked our relationship. I hope, through this letter, she can feel the depth of my heart, the tenderness and compassion I carry for her still. It is a conversation across time and space, a bridge between past and present, mother and daughter, spirit to spirit.

Love,

Junie

Dearest Mom,
   if you only knew...

It is fitting that this book of healing letters ends with a letter to you. You have shown up in many of the letters that I have written to others over my lifetime, but, until now, I haven't written to you, not since you passed away, leaving me unsettled in this world.

I loved you and hated you in equal measure at times. I was never enough, and then, at other times, I was everything. I learned at an early age to navigate your outbursts of love or anger, always on tender hooks for which side of you I would be subjected to. But I don't want this to be a letter of complaint or condemnation, as I have done so much deep work to find a place of only pure love and compassion in my heart for you, the complete and total you.

And so, in this healing letter, I wish to remember a time when I watched you step fully into love, when Papa lay dying and you couldn't, wouldn't let go—until you did, and in witnessing this, I found my own courage to let go too.

I remember us sitting by Papa's bedside, watching to see if he was still breathing. Day after day. Family coming and going. Sometimes we spoke to one another; other times, we were lost in our own worlds, unconnected in almost every way, except for the blood ties that brought us there. He had only been in a coma for a few days, and the doctors were talking about taking him off life support, pulling the plug.

After the shock wore off, it seemed the reasonable, even compassionate thing to do, for everyone except you. Dad had been dying for almost two years. Even still, I understood your resistance, your terror of him leaving you after forty-eight years of marriage. But, the thing was, Mom, he had already left you, and it would have been so much easier for the rest of us, for me, if you could have acknowledged this.

But you couldn't acknowledge this. "Don't you bring those funeral faces to my door!" you started demanding months before. This was even before Dad had begun to look feeble and gaunt, the cancer eating him up from the inside. "Where there is life, there is hope," you declared over and over again, as if to convince yourself of a truth that you hardly believed yourself.

But I had already started to grieve, walking around with a permanent lump in my throat and a tightness in my chest that wouldn't go away. But I couldn't come to you with my feelings, my grief, or my anger at the unfairness of it all. You wouldn't hear any of it, and so, as so often in my life, you couldn't be there for me when I needed you so badly.

In front of Papa, we only spoke lovingly. Some of us stayed with him all day long. Do you remember that Howard never left Papa's side? He held Papa's hand from morning to night. His only son. The one he never saw eye-to-eye with. Others came after work, his other children, grandchildren, sisters, and his one remaining brother. We'd tell each other stories of our days, at times slipping into memories of Papa. Sometimes we laughed and joked, then, as if it were wrong to do so, we'd retreat into silence and go our separate ways again.

We all wanted to bring as much love as possible into the room of a dying man. I don't know how much of this love you were able to let in, Mom, but for me, it dissolved any of the distance we may have felt between each other, as though death could bring us together, if only for a short time. The anger, resentment, none of it mattered there. I basked in the love because I knew that all too soon it would end, and we'd go back to our separate lives and unhealed hearts.

It seemed to me that fear, pain, and anger fueled your heart and kept you on your feet. This may be what you needed to feel rather than collapsing in a pile of pain on the floor. You were adamant that he would live, no matter what his condition.

"Where there is life, there is hope!" you would insist, time and again. Gently, and away from his room, we would try to dissuade you, "Think of Dad, Mom. He's in pain. He's got so little fight, and he's so tired. Try to let him go."

I don't know whether it was our words of support and love that shifted something for you, or you came to it on your own, but ten minutes before Dad took his last breath, and he opened his eyes, your heart must have opened or softened. His eyes were as clear as stars and were only for you, so full of love. I have never witnessed anything more beautiful, more remarkable in my life.

You took his hand so gently in your own and said, "I love you, Jimmy. I love you so much. What are you trying to tell me? That you love me too. I know you do, darling. Your children are all here. I'm going to be fine, sweetheart. Truly, I am. You do what you must and know that our love will always be with you."

Tears fell softly from Papa's eyes. He couldn't speak, couldn't move. But the love expressed in his eyes said more than words could ever hope to do. I wasn't sure if I believed in miracles before this, but no one could convince me now that miracles don't exist. I know Papa woke from his coma to say goodbye to you, to all of us. Inasmuch as you were able to let him go, he had to let you go as well.

Where there is life, there is hope. Where there is death, there can be peace.

I hope with all of my heart that wherever you are now, Mom, that you and Papa are together, in peace and in love.

With all my love,

Junie

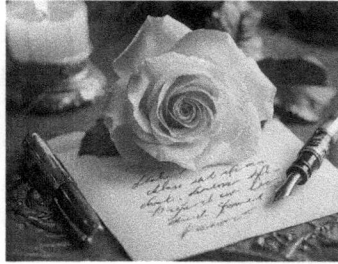

Dearest Reader,
  if you only knew...

Hello, I'm Megan Edge, a dear friend, coach, editor, and Junie's Healer.

When Junie and I began preparing her letters for this book, we knew the process would be about more than just selecting words for print. She had written dozens of letters over the years—letters to family members, lovers, friends, God, Death, and even to Cancer itself. Each was a testament to her courage, vulnerability, and truth-telling. As we sat together in her hospice room, the soft afternoon light spilling across the bed, we began the process of choosing which letters would appear in these pages.

It was an intimate and sacred act. We read each letter aloud, pausing to honor the emotions they stirred. Some letters carried a charge—a story still alive and needed for the book. Others felt complete, as though they had done their work in her life and no longer needed to remain in physical form. When that became clear, we set those letters aside for release. This was not simply "decluttering." It was an energetic choice to free her heart and her space from what no longer served her healing journey. It was at this point that we knew there needed to be a section of the book that spoke about the healing power of letting go, with the therapeutic power of letter writing and releasing.

Together, we created a small but significant ritual of letting go. Junie tore each unwanted letter into small pieces, her hands steady despite her illness. The sound of paper tearing was sharp and satisfying—a physical sign of release. I gathered the fragments and carried them not just out of her room, but out of the building entirely, ensuring the energy of those words would not linger in her space. She exhaled deeply as I returned, her face softer, her shoulders lighter.

"We need to share what we just did in the book," Junie said to me.

And so, here it is:

A Five-Step Sacred Ritual for Letting Go of Unwanted Letters

- Prepare the Space: Choose a quiet, comfortable place where you feel safe. Light a candle, play soft music, cuddle up in a favorite blanket, or include objects that hold meaning for you.
- Set Your Intention: Before beginning, speak aloud or silently why you are letting go of these letters. For example: "I release what no longer serves me. I keep the lessons, and I let go of the rest."
- Read and Witness: Read each letter one final time. Acknowledge the emotions it carries and any healing it has already brought. If possible, have a trusted friend or loved one witness this step.
- Release Through Destruction: Tear, shred, or burn the letter in a safe way, imagining the emotional weight leaving your body with each motion.
- Remove and Clear: Dispose of the remains outside of your living space. You may also wish to open a window, smudge with sage, or ring a bell to clear any lingering energy.

This is why it works:

The healing effects of writing letters—even those never sent—are well-documented in therapeutic research. Expressive writing has been shown to improve mood, strengthen immune function, and reduce stress by helping people process and make sense of emotionally charged experiences. In therapeutic letter writing, the act of addressing someone or something directly, without the pressure of a reply, can release suppressed emotions and restore a sense of agency.

Equally important is the intentional destruction of letters when their work is complete. Psychologists note that symbolic acts like tearing or burning can serve as a physical embodiment of letting go, helping to break the emotional ties to past hurts. In grief therapy and trauma recovery, such rituals are used to mark closure and transition, often leaving participants feeling lighter and more at peace. For those facing advanced illness, this process can be a way of reclaiming choice, shaping one's narrative, and creating emotional space for the present moment.

In the end, every letter—whether kept, shared, or released—becomes part of the tapestry of a life. By choosing which stories remain and which are set free, we not only honor the past but also make space for peace in the present.

This is the gift of the healing letter.

Blessings to you on your healing journey,

Love,

Megan

"May the pages you keep remind you who you are,
and the pages you let go remind you who
you no longer need to be."

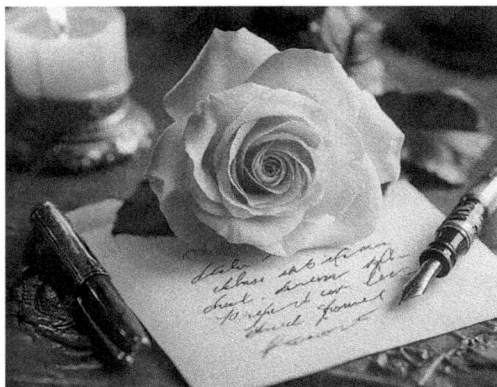

Post Script:

Junie passed away peacefully in the early hours on September 3, 2025. In the afternoon on the day before her death, I was able to lay in her hands the special copy of her book, complete with its cover, that I printed for her.

Although she was in a deep, pre-death sleep, she slightly opened her eyes and let out a big sigh. She knew. She knew we had completed If You Only Knew: A Book of Healing Letters, and it was now time for her to go.

Rest in peace, Junie

Love Megan

References

Pennebaker, J.W., & Smyth, J.M. (2016). Opening Up by Writing It Down. Guilford Press.

Neimeyer, R.A. (2012). Techniques of Grief Therapy. Routledge.

Trauma Research UK. (2024). Healing through Unsent Letters. Retrieved from traumaresearchuk.org

Therapist Aid. (2023). Letter Writing in Therapy. Retrieved from therapistaid.com

Island Narrative Therapy. (2024). Therapeutic Letter Writing. Retrieved from islandnarrativetherapy.ca

About the Author,
By the Author, MOI!

In my inimitable fashion—not short—it's a story. Go grab a cuppa tea.

So, you really want to know more about me and why I've been facilitating sacred writing circles for over three decades when getting a steady job would have been far more lucrative?

Okay, here goes:

Possibly because I'm bipolar and don't always make rational decisions! However, more in keeping with the truth, it's because I am passionate about writing and want to share my excitement with people who share my passion for writing. And I couldn't have continued year after year if I didn't see rewarding results time and time again.

One of the biggest turning points of my life came because of writing my play that exposed the fact that I have bipolar illness and the terror I felt about being judged. I fought my way through the pages of many journals until I finally surrendered to the bigger truth that my story needed to be told—not just because of what it could do for me but for countless others who suffer from the same illness.

Madness, Masks, and Miracles depict the madness or the dark night of the soul, I believe we all face while trying to find our way in life, the masks we wear to hide the madness, pain, shame, fear, heartbreak, and the miracles that allow us to take off our masks and be real.

Years later, I penned and published *Re-Write Your Life: A Transformational Guide to Writing and Healing the Stories of Our Lives* so that others could experience liberation through a conscious writing process.

Imagine if they gave hospital patients a steady supply of journals to do the same. And imagine if one of the mandates of the caregivers was to sit and have a conversation with each patient—perhaps even listening to what they wrote, paying full attention to their needs, and offering understanding and compassion. "Oh my," as Louis Armstrong so beautifully sang out, "What a wonderful world this could be."

Some people have accused me of living my life with rose-colored glasses, not seeing reality as it is. When I would succumb to those comments because it was too hard to be me, I would let my spirit die. Luckily, my journal would rescue me and bring me back to life. I would then equip those people with pen and paper and coerce them to follow my lead. I now have a back-end business selling rose-coloured glasses, pens, and paper—and making a fortune—and writing books like this one!

Shall I take your order now?

Resources

As you close the pages of *If You Only Knew: A Book of Healing Letters*, you may find yourself reflecting on your own journey of healing. Letter writing, as we've seen throughout these stories, is both deeply personal and profoundly universal. Healing, however, is rarely a solitary path. Support, understanding, and community are vital companions along the way.

The following resources are offered to guide you, whether you are seeking immediate help, exploring mental health support, or learning more about the healing power of writing. May these organizations, books, and studies serve as lanterns on your path.

Suicide Prevention and Crisis Support
National Suicide Prevention Lifeline (U.S.)
Call 988 or visit: https://988lifeline.org

Crisis Services Canada
Phone: 1-833-456-4566 or text 45645 |
https://www.crisisservicescanada.ca

Samaritans (U.K. & Ireland)
Phone: 116 123 | https://www.samaritans.org

Lifeline (Australia)
Phone: 13 11 14 | https://www.lifeline.org.au

Understanding Mental Illness
National Alliance on Mental Illness (NAMI)
https://nami.org

Mind (U.K.)
https://www.mind.org.uk
Canadian Mental Health Association (CMHA)
https://cmha.ca

Caregiver Support
Family Caregiver Alliance
www.caregiver.org

Caregiver Action Network
www.caregiveraction.org

Alzheimer Society of Canada
www.alzheimer.ca

The Healing Power of Writing
Bolton, Gillie.

The Therapeutic Potential of Creative Writing: Writing Myself.
Pennebaker, James W.

Opening Up by Writing It Down: How Expressive Writing Improves Health and Eases Emotional Pain.
Adams, Kathleen.

Journal to the Self: Twenty-Two Paths to Personal Growth.
Neimeyer, Robert A. (Ed.).

Techniques of Grief Therapy: Creative Practices for Counseling the Bereaved.

Closing Note

You are not alone. Whether you are a writer, a caregiver, or someone finding their way through the landscapes of loss and healing, may these resources remind you of the strength that comes from reaching out, the courage that grows from sharing your truth, and the grace that is found in every healing letter.

Other Books by the Author

Your Life Matters: 8 Simple Steps to Writing Your Story

"For those with a burning desire to write their memoir, Junie torches every negative emotion, cuts through the harsh inner critic who sets up our self-imposed obstacles and illuminates the pathway to liberation. Junie sets the stage for the freedom to reveal the life stories that will make a fabulously interesting journey of self-discovery for the writer as well as the reader. Brilliant!"
~ **Judith Rockert**

Re-Write Your Life: A Transformational Guide to Writing and Healing the Stories of Our Lives

"Junie Swadron is both a guide and a muse. Her book is a bright lantern, illuminating the often dark and tricky terrain of the soul. Grounded in personal experience, her techniques catalyze the deep authenticity possible to us all."
~ **Julia Cameron**, author of The Artist's Way.

Madness, Masks and Miracles: A Play to Dispel Myths and Stigmas about Mental Illness ~ Co-written by Junie Swadron & Victoria Maxwell

"This play is a winner. June Swadron and her writing team and actors engage the audience immediately and throughout with what it's like to have a mental illness in contemporary society. We feel the anguish and confusion, we witness the denial in co-workers and family, we experience the shame of the sufferer and the multiple losses, and we learn painfully about the limitations of our treatments. Yet this production is not cynical or depressing. It is moving, inspiring, and intensely evocative. A gift. A call-to-arms. A must-see for every Canadian citizen."
~ **Dr. Michael Meyers**, President of the Canadian Psychiatric Association

Colouring Your Dreams Come True: A Bedtime Story and Colouring Book for Children of All Ages and the Child within Every Adult

Jazzy's Miracle Mission: A True Story Colouring Book

www.ingramcontent.com/pod-product-compliance
Lightning Source LLC
Chambersburg PA
CBHW051727090426
42738CB00010B/2135